my **revisi⊕n** notes

AQA AS/A-level History

TSARIST AND COMMUNIST RUSSIA

1855–1964

Michael Scott-Baumann

Series editor
David Ferriby

HODDER
EDUCATION
AN HACHETTE UK COMPANY

Acknowledgements

The Publishers would like to thank the following for permission to reproduce copyright material.

pp.9, 11, 19, 43, 71, 89 *Rulers and Subjects: Government and People in Russia, 1801–1991* by John Gooding (1996) Copyright © 1996 by Bloomsbury Publishing Plc; **pp.19, 21, 29, 51, 61** From *A People's Tragedy: The Russian Revolution 1891–1924* by Orlando Figes (1996). © Penguin Books; **pp.19, 29, 69, 87** From *Russia: A 1,000-Year Chronicle of the Wild East* by Martin Sixsmith (2012). Copyright © Random House; **pp.29, 48, 51, 81** From *A History of Modern Russia* by Robert Service (1997). Copyright © Penguin; **pp.35, 39, 41, 61, 85, 92** From *Russia: The Tsarist and Soviet Legacy* by Edward Acton (1995), © Taylor & Francis. Used by permission; **pp.55, 69, 75, 92** From D. Volkogonov (1999), *The Rise and Fall of the Soviet Empire*. Published by HarperCollins UK; **pp.61, 77, 92** From *The Soviet Achievement* by J. P. Nettl © by J. P. Nettl (1967). Reprinted by kind permission of Thames & Hudson, Ltd., London; **pp.63, 65, 69, 87** *Revolutionary Russia, 1891–1991: A History* by Orlando Figes. Published by Penguin Books.

Hodder Education would like to thank Sally Waller who wrote the previous edition of this revision guide.

Every effort has been made to trace all copyright holders, but if any have been inadvertently overlooked, the Publishers will be pleased to make the necessary arrangements at the first opportunity.

Although every effort has been made to ensure that website addresses are correct at time of going to press, Hodder Education cannot be held responsible for the content of any website mentioned in this book. It is sometimes possible to find a relocated web page by typing in the address of the home page for a website in the URL window of your browser.

Hachette UK's policy is to use papers that are natural, renewable and recyclable products and made from wood grown in sustainable forests. The logging and manufacturing processes are expected to conform to the environmental regulations of the country of origin.

Orders: please contact Bookpoint Ltd, 130 Milton Park, Abingdon, Oxon OX14 4SE. Telephone: +44 (0)1235 827720. Fax: +44 (0)1235 400454. Email education@bookpoint. co.uk Lines are open from 9 a.m. to 5 p.m., Monday to Saturday, with a 24-hour message answering service. You can also order through our website: www.hoddereducation.co.uk

ISBN: 978 1 4718 7616 5

© Michael Scott-Baumann

First published in 2017 by

Hodder Education,
An Hachette UK Company
Carmelite House
50 Victoria Embankment
London EC4Y 0DZ

www.hoddereducation.co.uk

Impression number   10 9 8 7 6 5 4 3 2 1

Year   2020 2019 2018 2017

Cover photo © Alex_Mac-Fotolia

Illustrations by Integra

Typeset by Integra Software Services Pvt. Ltd., Pondicherry, India

Printed in Spain

A catalogue record for this title is available from the British Library.

My revision planner

Part 2 The Soviet Union, 1917–64 (A-level only)

Introduction

Component 1: Breadth study

Component 1 involves the study of significant developments over an extended period of time (around 50 years at AS and 100 years at A-level) and an evaluation of historical interpretations.

Tsarist and Communist Russia, 1855–1964

The specification lists the content of Tsarist and Communist Russia in two parts, each part being divided into two sections.

Part 1   Autocracy, reform and revolution: Russia, 1855–1917
- Trying to preserve autocracy, 1855–94
- The collapse of autocracy, 1894–1917

Part 2   The Soviet Union, 1917–64
- The emergence of communist dictatorship, 1917–41
- The Stalinist dictatorship and reaction, 1941–64

Although each period of study is set out in chronological sections in the specification, an exam question may arise from one or more of these sections.

The AS examination

The AS examination, which you may be taking, includes all the content in Part 1.

You are required to answer:
- Section A: one question on two contrasting interpretations: which interpretation is the more convincing? You need to identify the arguments in each extract and assess how convincing they are, using your knowledge, and then reach a judgement on which is the more convincing. The question is worth 25 marks.
- Section B: one essay question out of two. The questions will be set on a broad topic, reflecting the fact that this is a breadth paper, and will require you to analyse whether you agree or disagree with a statement. Almost certainly, you will be doing both and reaching a balanced conclusion. The question is worth 25 marks.

The exam lasts one and a half hours, and you should spend about equal time on each section.

At AS, Component 1 will be worth a total of 50 marks and 50 per cent of AS examination.

The A-level examination

The A-level examination at the end of the course includes all the content of both parts.

You are required to answer:
- Section A: one question on three interpretations: how convincing is each interpretation? You are NOT required to reach a conclusion about which might be the most convincing. You need to identify the arguments in each extract and use your knowledge to assess how convincing each one is. The question is worth 30 marks.
- Section B: two essay questions out of three. The questions will be set on a broad topic (usually covering 20–25 years). The question styles will vary but they will all require you to analyse factors and reach a conclusion. The focus may be on causation, or consequence, or continuity and change. Each question in this section is worth 25 marks.

The exam lasts two and a half hours. You should spend about one hour on Section A and about 45 minutes on each of the two essays.

At A-level, Component 1 will be worth a total of 80 marks and 40 per cent of A-level examination.

In both the AS and A-level examinations you are being tested on the ability to:
- use relevant historical information (Sections A and B)
- evaluate different historical interpretations (Section A)
- analyse factors and reach a judgement (Section B).

How to use this book

This book has been designed to help you develop the knowledge and skills necessary to succeed in the examination.

- The book is divided into four sections – one for each section of the A-level specification.
- Each section is made up of a series of topics organised into double-page spreads.
- On the left-hand page you will find a summary of the key content you will need to learn.
- Words in bold in the key content are defined in the glossary (see pages 95–96).
- On the right-hand page you will find exam-focused activities.

Together, these two strands of the book will provide you with the knowledge and skills essential for examination success.

▼ **Key historical content**

▼ **Exam-focused activities**

Examination activities

There are three levels of examination-focused activities:

- Band 1 activities are designed to develop the foundation skills needed to pass the exam. These have a green heading and this symbol:
- Band 2 activities are designed to build on the skills developed in Band 1 activities and to help you to achieve a C grade. These have an orange heading and this symbol:
- Band 3 activities are designed to enable you to access the highest grades. These have a purple heading and this symbol:

Some of the activities have answers or suggested answers on pages 99–104. These have the following symbol to indicate this:

Each section ends with an examination-style question and sample answers with commentary. This will give you guidance on what is expected to achieve the top grade.

You can also keep track of your revision by ticking off each topic heading in the book, or by ticking the checklist on the contents page. Tick each box when you have:

- revised and understood a topic
- completed the activities.

Mark schemes

For some of the activities in the book it will be useful to refer to the mark schemes for this paper. Below are abbreviated forms.

Section A – Interpretations

Level	AS-level examination	A-level examination
1	Unsupported, vague or general comments. Little understanding of the interpretations. (1–5)	Mostly general or vague comments *or* shows an accurate understanding of one extract only. (1–6)
2	Partial understanding of the interpretations. Undeveloped comments with a little knowledge. (6–10)	Some accurate comments on interpretations given in at least two of the extracts. Some analysis, but little evaluation. (7–12)
3	Reasonable understanding of interpretations. Some knowledge to support arguments. (11–15)	Some supported comments on the three interpretations with comments on strength, with some analysis and evaluation. (13–18)
4	Good understanding of interpretations. A supported conclusion, but not all comments well substantiated and judgements may be limited. (16–20)	Good understanding of the interpretations, combined with knowledge of historical context, with mostly well-supported evaluation but minor limitations in depth and breadth. (19–24)
5	Good understanding of interpretations. Thorough evaluation of extracts, leading to a well-substantiated judgement. (21–25)	Very good understanding of interpretations, combined with strong awareness of historical context to analyse and evaluate with well-supported arguments. (25–30)

Section B – Essays

Level	AS-level examination	A-level examination
1	Extremely limited or irrelevant information. Unsupported, vague or generalising comments. (1–5)	Extremely limited or irrelevant information. Unsupported, vague or generalising comments. (1–5)
2	Descriptive or partial, failing to grasp full demands of question. Limited in scope. (6–10)	Descriptive or partial, failing to grasp full demands of question. Limited in scope. (6–10)
3	Some understanding and answer is adequately organised. Information showing understanding of some key features. (11–15)	Understanding of question and a range of largely accurate information showing awareness of key issues and features, but lacking in precise detail. Some balance established. (11–15)
4	Understanding shown with range of largely accurate information showing awareness of some key issues and features, leading to a limited judgement. (16–20)	Good understanding of question. Well organised and effectively communicated with range of clear and specific supporting information showing good understanding of key features and issues, with some conceptual awareness. (16–20)
5	Good understanding. Well organised and effectively communicated. Range of clear information showing good understanding and some conceptual awareness. Analytical in style, leading to a substantiated judgement. (21–25)	Very good understanding of full demands of question. Well organised and effectively delivered, with well-selected, precise supporting information. Fully analytical with balanced argument and well-substantiated judgement. (21–25)

1 Trying to preserve autocracy, 1855–94

Political authority and the state of Russia

REVISED

Background

Mid-nineteenth century Russia was a large but economically underdeveloped empire with a ratio of village to town dwellers of 11:1. Around 85 per cent of the population were illiterate peasants, mostly either privately or state-owned **serfs**. Most serfs belonged to village communes, or **mirs**, where their village elders regulated their primitive strip-farming. They paid their master for the land in rent or labour and could be bought, sold and beaten by him.

In 1855, Russia was an empire ruled by an **autocratic** Tsar. The **Tsar** was also the head of the Russian **Orthodox Church**. He was believed to possess semi-divine powers. His edicts were law and he could choose his own advisers.

The impact of the Crimean War

Alexander II became Tsar in March 1855. Russia was in the final stage of a disastrous war in the Crimea (north of the Black Sea). They had been fighting the British, French and Turkish there since 1853 and had suffered several defeats, including the Battles of Balaclava and Inkerman in 1854. In August 1855, they lost Sebastopol, a major naval base. The final defeat in 1856 highlighted both the problem of Russia's reliance on serf armies (where harshly treated **conscripts** served for 25 years) and the country's economic backwardness, particularly its lack of railways and outdated weaponry. Despite spending 45 per cent of annual expenditure on the army, Russia suffered incompetent officers, humiliation and an increase in serf uprisings.

Alexander II and the background to emancipation

Having travelled the empire, served on his father's Council of State and led a **serfdom** committee, Alexander II believed in serf **emancipation** to curb tensions and stimulate the economy. His brother, Grand Duke Constantine, and his aunt, Grand Duchess Elena Pavlovna, as well as other enlightened **bureaucrats**, such as the brothers, **Nicholas** and **Dmitri Milyutin**, shared his views.

Motives for reform

There were numerous motives – political, economic and intellectual – behind Alexander II's reforms.

Political motives

Tsarist autocracy depended on the nobility, yet many nobles who traditionally shunned business and relied on serfs to make money out of their estates were in heavy debt. A growing serf population and inadequate agricultural systems meant declining incomes, and many had been forced to **mortgage** their land and even their serfs as security for loans from the state bank. Younger nobles had become apathetic, demotivated and critical of the regime.

Economic motives

Serfdom kept the peasants in the mirs, preventing them from moving to work in town factories and keeping the internal demand for goods low. The traditional practices of the mir prevented experimentation with new agricultural methods, and rural poverty left many serfs unable to pay their taxes. Consequently, by 1859, the state faced a debt of 54 million roubles.

Moral and intellectual motives

Westernisers believed that Russia should abandon serfdom, imitating Western Europe, while **Slavophiles** favoured reforming serfdom but wanted to keep Russia's traditional peasant society. Some **intellectuals** presented the moral case against treating people like animals, while 'nihilists' believed in sweeping away all tradition – including autocracy.

! Summarise the arguments

Read the following interpretation on the reasons for Russia's backwardness. Summarise the main arguments, as opposed to the facts, and rephrase them in your own words.

EXTRACT A

Adapted from John Gooding, Rulers and Subjects: Government and People in Russia, 1801–1991 *(1996)*

Russia lacked the economic, cultural and technological base to remain a great power in the mid-nineteenth century, and was more backward now than at the beginning of the century. In the intervening years Western Europe had developed by leaps and bounds – the triumphs of its new technology and its middle-class would be celebrated at the great exhibitions of the 1850s. Russia, however, had neither, having fallen behind by the deliberate choice of its ruler and ruling class. The Crimean disaster resulted in the first place from technological weakness; there were no railways to transport troops and supplies to the distant Crimea, and the army lacked up-to-date artillery and equipment. [However,] the poor performance of the armed forces in the Crimea pointed to much more in fact than technological weakness. The armed forces would not again become an effective shield without all-round modernisation of Russian life, and that in turn was incompatible with crude repression. If the country was to remain a great power it could not depend solely upon its own resources and its supposed innate virtues; it would have to open itself once more to the West, to learn not only the techniques but something of the ways of life and thought which had found reflection in the armed superiority of Britain and France.

¡ Identify an argument

Below is a sample question which asks how far you agree with a specific statement, followed by two paragraphs in response. One suggests a high-level answer because it advances a supported argument (a view supported by reasoning and fact). The other suggests a low-level answer because it contains only description (facts but not in support of a view) and assertion (a view not supported by reasoning and fact). Identify which is which.

'Russia's failure in the Crimean War was the sole reason why Alexander II was interested in reform after 1855.' Explain whether you agree or disagree with this view.

Answer 1

Although Russia entered the Crimean War in 1853, confident of victory, its hopes had rapidly been dashed in a series of disastrous military defeats. It was humiliated at the Battles of Balaclava and Inkerman in 1854 and, worse still, in 1855, Russia's Black Sea naval base at Sebastopol was captured. Russia's army was reliant on peasant conscripts who served for 25 years and were subject to brutal military discipline. The commanders were poor and there was a very limited railway system. Military weapons were outdated and Russia lacked the industrial capacity to supply its troops. The huge army used up around 45 per cent of the government's annual expenditure while Russia's outdated social system maintained serfdom and there were many peasant uprisings during the Crimean War. The war was the main reason for Alexander II's interest in reform after 1855.

Answer 2

Russia's failures in the Crimea certainly added to Alexander II's personal desire for change in Russia. He came to the throne shortly before Russia's defeat at Sebastopol in 1855 and he was acutely aware of the humiliating inadequacies the war had thrown up. Armies of serf conscripts had proved unreliable, generals incompetent and the economy unable to support the military effort. The dangers of peasant revolt were particularly frightening for an autocratic ruler. The war had also increased demands from intellectuals to tackle the outdated system of serfdom, while reformers, such as Dmitri Milyutin, with whom Alexander associated, argued for modernisation. The need to reform in order to strengthen the state and prevent a repetition of this recent disaster must have weighed heavily on Alexander II's mind in 1855.

Political authority and attempts at reform: emancipation of the serfs and its impact

REVISED

Procedure

After the **Crimean War** ended in March 1856, Alexander set up committees to examine emancipation and in 1858–59 he toured the country delivering pro-emancipation speeches. However, the provincial nobles failed to agree on measures and Alexander was exasperated by the prolonged debate, which took place against a background of escalating peasant unrest. Finally, he established a commission of 38, led by Nicholas Milyutin, to produce the final measure.

The emancipation of the serfs was proclaimed in Alexander's Edict of 1861. It only applied to the privately owned serfs. The state serfs received their freedom in 1866. It permitted some greater modernisation of the economy but its terms were not as 'liberating' in practice as its supporters had anticipated.

Terms of the Edict	Assessment and significance
• Serfs were declared 'free' and could marry who they chose, own property, set up businesses, travel and enjoy legal rights. • Serfs were given their own cottage and an allotment of land.	• Enterprising peasants could buy up land, increase output and make money from the sale of surplus grain. • Those prepared to sell land could move to an industrialising city and obtain regular wages. • Land allocations varied; for some, these were insufficient to live on. • Peasant 'rights' often remained theoretical because of the other terms of the Edict, e.g. freedom to travel.
• Landlords were granted government bonds as compensation.	• Landowners could use compensation to redeem debts and invest in industrial enterprises. • Some could only just pay off debts and were forced to sell their remaining land.
• Serfs were required to make 49 annual 'redemption payments' for the land they were given.	• Redemption payments provoked unrest. • Land prices were sometimes fixed above market value, leaving freed serfs in considerable debt. • Some peasants had to work for their old masters or rent land from them (paid back with crops) to survive. • The 'purchasing power' of the peasants remained low; some became drifting landless labourers.
• The mir was responsible for the collection of taxes, including redemption dues. • Freed serfs had to remain within the mir until the redemption payments were complete. • The mir supervised the farming of allocated land.	• Mirs constrained the peasants, preventing them from leaving the countryside. • Mirs tended to promote restrictive and backward farming practices.
• Landowners were allowed to retain meadows, pasture, woodland and personal land. • Communal open fields were controlled by the mir for use by everyone.	• Some former serfs struggled to make a living without the use of additional land. • Serfs lost their landlords' 'protection'.
• The obruk (labour service) remained for a two-year period of 'temporary obligation'.	• Peasants were resentful; there were 647 peasant riots in four months after the decree.

Complete the paragraph

Below is a sample essay question and the outline of a paragraph written in answer to the question. The paragraph begins with a relevant comment in relation to the question and ends with a further link. However, it lacks supporting examples. Complete the paragraph by providing some factual detail in the space provided.

'The Emancipation Edict of 1861 was successful in improving the lives of the Russian peasants by 1881.' To what extent do you agree with this view?

> Although the 1861 Edict gave the freed serfs many legal freedoms, such as the right to marry who they chose, run businesses, own property and travel, in many respects the Russian peasants were little better off.
>
> _____
>
> Consequently, methods of farming did not significantly improve and the number of serfs able to travel to nearby towns and work in industry was limited. This restricted the opportunities the Edict might have been expected to give the peasants in order to improve their standard of living.

Interpretation: content or argument?

Read the following interpretation on the impact of emancipation on the peasants and the two alternative answers to the question. Which answer focuses more on the content and which focuses more on the arguments of the interpretation? Explain your answer.

With reference to your understanding of the historical context, assess how convincing the arguments in this extract are in relation to the impact of emancipation on the peasants.

Answer 1

This extract states that, although the serfs gained certain rights, such as to own property and to marry without permission, they had to continue to work for the landowners for two years. Also, the peasants' land was given to the commune which would still control the peasants' lives. This shows that the peasants were still not completely free.

Answer 2

This extract acknowledges that the serfs gained certain legal freedoms, such as the right to own property and marry without permission. However, it argues that the serfs were still highly restricted. Their rights were severely limited, especially for the next two years, during which they would continue to have to 'fulfil their former obligations'. The author argues that, as a result, the peasants were far less free than their European counterparts. Also, the land taken from the landowners was put under the control of the communes and they, not the peasants, decided how the land would be farmed.

EXTRACT A

Adapted from John Gooding, Rulers and Subjects: Government and People in Russia, 1801–1991 _(1996)_

The serfs remained disadvantaged, and their freedom was so circumscribed that to many Europeans it might not have seemed like freedom at all. True, they were to enjoy the rights of free persons – to own property, for example, and to marry without permission, and in general to shape their lives without regard to the landowners. But these rights were only for the future. For the next two years, the existing order was to remain: the ex-serfs would have to be 'obedient towards their nobles and scrupulously fulfil their former obligations', and the lords would keep their police powers over them ...

A further limitation of the peasant's 'freedom' was that the land transferred from the lord would be allotted not to him but to the community as a whole. As a result he could not farm independently even if he wanted to, and the communal agricultural system would continue as before. The elders and officials of the commune would in fact have to replace the lord.

Political authority and attempts at reform: Alexander's other reforms

Reasons for further reform

- There was disappointment at the emancipation measure on the part of peasants and landlords, with continued unrest in the countryside.
- The emancipation left issues needing resolution, e.g. conscription and control of local government and justice.

The main reforms and their success

Military reforms, 1874

- Conscription (for those over 20 years old) was made compulsory for all classes.
- Length of service was reduced from 25 to 15 years, nine years of which were spent 'in reserve'.
- Welfare improvements, e.g. the abolition of corporal punishment and army service was no longer to be given as a punishment.
- Military colleges were established to train officers.
- Modern weaponry was introduced.

Assessment of succcess

- A smaller but better-trained army was created.
- Costs of the military to the government were reduced.
- Literacy was improved through army education campaigns.
- Officers were still mainly aristocrats and the upper classes served less time, or 'bought' their way out of service.
- In the war against Turkey from 1877 to 1878, victory took longer than expected; in 1914, Russia suffered defeat.

Local government reforms, 1864 and 1870

- Rural councils (known as **Zemstva**) were established at district and provincial levels (1864).
- Councils were to be elected through an indirect system giving an initial vote to the nobles, townspeople, Church and peasants but weighted in favour of the nobility.
- Zemstva were given power to improve public services, including relief for the poor, and to develop industry.

Assessment of succcess

- Zemstva offered some representative government at local level.
- They were dominated by nobles and 'professionals'; peasants had limited influence.
- They made significant improvements in welfare and education.
- They provided a forum for debate on, and criticism of, government policies.

- They had no control over taxation and law and order. Tsarist-appointed provincial governors could overturn their decisions.

Judicial reforms, 1864

- The reforms established a single system of local, provincial and national courts.
- Criminal cases were before barristers and a jury.
- All classes were judged equal before the law and proceedings were open to the public and reporters.
- Judges' training and pay were improved.

Assessment of succcess

- A fairer and less corrupt system was created.
- The jury system could undermine government control, e.g. in the case of Vera Zasulich, who was acquitted of terrorism, although guilty. As a result, from 1878, political crimes were tried in special courts.
- Ecclesiastical and military courts continued and the reform was not applicable to Poland.

Educational reform (1863–64)

Improving standards of literacy and numeracy were necessary for Russia's modernisation. The **liberal**-minded minister Alexander Golovnin led some important changes:
- The Zemstva took responsibility for primary education (replacing the Church).
- Free primary education was made available to all – regardless of class and sex.
- New vocational schools were set up at secondary level.
- Students from both types of secondary school could progress to university.
- Universities were made self-governing in 1863 and began offering broader and more liberal courses.

Strengths of the reforms

Between 1856 and 1880:
- The number of primary schools tripled.
- The number of children in primary education more than doubled.
- There was a greater selection of subjects – for girls as well as boys.
- The number of students at university tripled.

Problems with the reforms

- The primary curriculum was still based on religion and offered basic reading, writing and arithmetic.
- Secondary education was still fee-paying so was limited to the better-off.
- More **radical** students joined opposition movements committed to violence.

! Delete as applicable
a

Below is a sample essay question and a paragraph written in answer to this question. Read the paragraph and decide which option (underlined) is the most appropriate. Delete the less appropriate options and complete the paragraph by justifying your selection.

> 'The military, local government and judicial reforms of 1864–74 were a direct result of the emancipation of the serfs.' Explain why you agree or disagree with this view.

The emancipation of the serfs was **the most important reason/an important reason/just one of many reasons** for the military, local government and judicial reforms of 1864–74. Serf emancipation meant that a new system of military recruitment was needed to replace serf conscription and that the landlords' jurisdiction in the countryside had to be replaced by a new arrangement. The establishment of rural councils and local courts **was in response to/was partly in response to/was connected with** the changes brought about by serf emancipation. This is because …

_____

_____

_____

_____

_____

╪ Eliminate irrelevance
a

Below is a sample essay question and a paragraph written in answer to it. Read the paragraph and identify parts that are not directly relevant or helpful to the question. Draw a line through the information that is irrelevant and justify your deletions in the margin.

> 'The reforms of Alexander II transformed Russian society between 1855 and 1881.' Assess the validity of this view.

Among the reforms that transformed Russian society were changes in education. The changes were introduced by Alexander II's Education Minister, Golovnin, who, like the Milyutin brothers, had liberal ideas. The educational changes came to an end when Golovnin was replaced by the conservative Tolstoy in 1866. In 1864, the new Zemstva were given responsibility for the provision of education in their own areas. These Zemstva were elected councils chosen by the nobles, townspeople, Church and peasants, although voting was arranged in a way that allowed the nobles more influence. The schools they established were made available to all, which helped transform society, even though the poor rarely got beyond primary level. Although the serfs had been emancipated in 1861, many were still very poor and reliant on subsistence farming. The educational curriculum was also expanded with new scientific subjects and vocational secondary schools offering opportunities for advancement. There was still a very small middle class in Russia though. The universities were given more control over the courses they offered. This transformed society by creating a new group of critical and radical students.

Government and Tsars: Alexander II, reaction and the emergence of opposition

REVISED

Reform and the spread of opposition

Alexander's reforms in the 1860s stimulated both excitement and the emergence of opposition.

- The relaxation of censorship laws encouraged the spread of more radical books.
- Educational changes led to the growth of more independent, radical student organisations.
- Legal reforms promoted legal careers and attracted the educated middle classes who were critical of government.

Opposition groups included:

- 1862: 'Young Russia', a student organisation which was hostile to both the Tsar and the Church. This group was probably responsible for a series of fires in **St Petersburg** in 1862.
- 1863: 'The Organisation', which was set up by students at Moscow University to co-ordinate revolutionary activities.

Alexander and reaction

Following assassination attempts on the Tsar in 1866 and 1867, a period of **reaction** set in.

Alexander appointed reactionary ministers, such as Dmitri Tolstoy and Peter Shuvalov, who argued that westernising changes were weakening Russia. So, although military and economic reforms continued, Alexander's other reforming impulses were halted, or even reversed.

Area	Policies	Results
Education	• Authority over primary schools was returned to the Church and the activities of the Zemstva were restricted. • Secondary schools were ordered to remove from the curriculum the sciences they had introduced. • Students from vocational schools could only go to higher technical institutions (1871), not university. • Subjects thought to encourage critical thought, such as literature and history, were banned in universities. • Student organisations were banned. • University appointments could be vetoed by the government.	• Religious control was reasserted. • The curriculum was restricted. • Female education declined. • Many students escaped restrictions by studying abroad. Here they were influenced by radical Russians living in exile.
Police and law courts	• The work of the Third Section (secret police) was increased. • Until 1878 political offenders could face **show trials**. • 1878: political crimes were tried in secret in military courts. • 1879: governor-generals were given emergency powers to use military courts and impose exile.	• Critics and opponents thrived underground. • The 'show trials' were abandoned after sympathetic juries acquitted the accused, e.g. Vera Zasulich (see page 12).

A change of heart?

The Russo-Turkish War (1877–78), famine (1879–80), the beginnings of an industrial recession and further assassination attempts in 1879 and 1880 led Alexander II to establish a commission under Count Loris-Melikov, who had been appointed Minister of the Interior in 1880 to investigate the spread of revolutionary activity. This led to the:

- release of political prisoners
- relaxation of censorship
- lifting of restrictions on the activities of the Zemstva
- removal of the tax on salt
- abolition of the Third Section (replaced by the **Okhrana**).

! Mind map

Use the information on the page opposite to add detail to the spider diagram below to show reasons for the emergence of opposition to Alexander II.

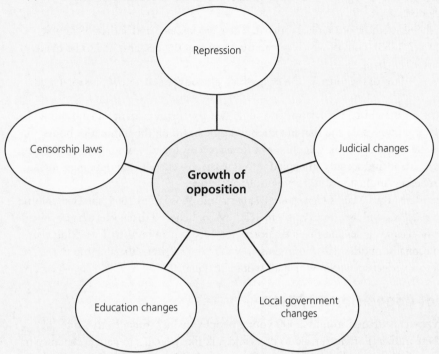

i Turning assertion into argument · a

Below is a sample essay question and a series of assertions. Read the question and then add a justification to each of the assertions to turn it into a supported view, so creating an argument.

'The emergence of opposition to the Tsarist regime was the result of the Tsar's own reforms.' Assess the validity of this view.

The growth of opposition was the result of Alexander's judicial reforms

_____

_____

The growth of opposition came about because Alexander II relaxed censorship

_____

_____

The growth of opposition was the result of Alexander's reform of education and the universities

_____

_____

Opposition: radical thinkers and populist opposition

Radical thinkers

Radical thinkers, whose works began to influence young and educated Russians to adopt socialist ideas, included:

- Nikolai Chernyshevsky, editor of a radical journal, *The Contemporary*, and author of a book, *What Is To Be Done?* (1863), both of which spread the view that the peasants had to be made leaders of revolutionary change.
- Alexander Herzen, editor of the journal *The Bell*, which also advocated a new peasant-based social structure.
- Mikhail Bakunin, an anarchist and socialist who suggested private ownership of land should be replaced by collective ownership and that income should be based on the number of hours worked. In 1869, he wrote the book *Catechism of a Revolutionary*, together with Sergei Nechaev. Published in Switzerland and secretly smuggled into Russia, this encouraged opponents of Tsardom to be merciless in the pursuit of revolutionary change.
- Bakunin also translated Karl Marx's *Communist Manifesto* into Russian in 1869; the first volume of Marx's *Das Kapital* was published in Russia in 1872. Marx believed that society had evolved through a series of class struggles and that a final struggle between an industrial working class (proletariat) and capitalist middle class (bourgeoisie) would, after a short 'dictatorship of the proletariat', lead to a perfect society in which all would be equal.

The spread of opposition 1870–81

- 1874: **Peter Lavrov** encouraged around 2,000 young people, mainly students, to 'go to the people'. These **Narodniks** (Populists) tried to dress and talk like peasants to gain acceptance in villages and spread their socialist ideas. However, ignorance, loyalty to the Church and to the Tsar and fear that the Narodniks were secret police agents led peasants to reject them and sometimes hand them over to the police. There were 1,600 arrests.
- 1876: a Second Narodnik movement was attempted but, like the first, it failed with many arrests.
- 1877: the remaining Narodniks established **Land and Liberty**, which had similar aims but also a commitment to assassination. Their efforts included:
  ○ the assassination of General Mezemstev, head of the Third Section, 1878
  ○ several attempts on the Tsar's life.
- In 1879, Land and Liberty split into:

The Black Partition	The People's Will
• Organised by Georgi Plekhanov • Aimed to 'partition the black (fertile) soil' provinces among the peasants • Worked peacefully among peasants • Spread radical materials among students and workers • Weakened by arrests in 1880–81 and broken up • Plekhanov later became a **Marxist**.	• Led by Timofei Mikhailov • Larger than the Black Partition • Advocated violent methods and assassination (particularly of the Tsar) • March 1881 – succeeded in assassinating Alexander II with a bomb as he was travelling by coach to the **Winter Palace** in St Petersburg.

Significance of the spread of opposition

- Government failures (e.g. the show trials) and assassinations helped suggest the Tsarist regime lacked authority.
- Demands for 'reform from below' had grown and spread socially and geographically.
- The conservative bureaucracy, nobles and landowners who had opposed Alexander's reforms forced him to adopt a more reactionary stance by linking reform to growing opposition.

Spot the mistake

a

Below is a sample exam question and a paragraph written in answer to the question. Why does this paragraph not earn high praise? What is wrong with the focus of the answer in this paragraph?

'How successful was opposition to the regime of Alexander II in the years from 1855 to 1881?'

Opposition to Alexander II achieved very little in the years from 1855 to 1881. Most of it was short-lived and was weakened by arrests. For instance, the Narodniks aroused the suspicion of the peasants and many of them were handed over to the police. Similarly, the Black Partition was severely weakened by arrests in 1880 and 1881. Although both groups were focused on winning peasant support, the vast majority of the peasantry were unmoved. Also, 'show trials' were implemented.

Spectrum of importance

Below is a sample AS-level exam question and a series of statements relevant to the question. Use your own knowledge and the information on the previous pages to reach a judgement about the importance of these points to the question posed.

Write numbers on the spectrum below to indicate the relative importance of the statements. Having done this, write a brief justification of your placement, explaining why some of these factors are more important than others. The resulting diagram could form the basis of an essay plan.

'During the course of Alexander's reign (1855–81), Tsarist authority was severely undermined by opposition groups.' Explain whether you agree or disagree with this view.

1 Young Russia was probably behind a series of fires in St Petersburg in 1862.

2 Socialist writings had a minority readership – mostly students and the liberal intelligentsia.

3 Marxism was discussed in underground reading circles.

4 Peasants were suspicious of the Narodniks and sometimes reported them to the police.

5 The head of the Third Section was assassinated.

6 Many members of the Black Partition were arrested from 1880 to 1881.

7 The People's Will assassinated Alexander II in March 1881.

Least important ←——————————————————————→ Most important

Political authority in action: Alexander III, Russification and the treatment of ethnic minorities and Jews

REVISED

The reassertion of autocracy

- After his father's assassination (see page 16), **Alexander III** ascended the throne and was crowned on 27 May 1881. He was advised by the reactionary **Konstantin Pobedonostev**, procurator of the Holy Synod. He encouraged the Tsar to reassert the principle of autocracy and abandon his father's reforms. The new Tsar announced: 'I shall be sole and absolute ruler, for a kingdom cannot be ruled without an iron hand. Only absolute power can safeguard Russia.'
- Alexander III arrested 150 members of the People's Will and publicly hanged those responsible for his father's assassination. He increased the powers of the police. He made the Department of Police, which supervised the Okhrana, responsible to the Ministry of Internal Affairs so that its activities could be monitored. Spies and counter-spies were also widely used.
- From 1882, any area of the empire could be deemed an 'area of subversion', with police agents able to arrest, imprison or exile on suspicion.
- In 1885, closed court sessions (where trials were held in secret) without juries were reintroduced.
- In 1889, Alexander III introduced **Land Captains**, appointed from the nobility. These replaced local magistrates and had the power to override Zemstva elections and decisions. They could overturn the judgements of local courts and order the flogging of peasants.
- In 1890, the peasant vote to the Zemstva was reduced.
- Outspoken liberal members of the judiciary and the Zemstva were removed from office.

Russification

Alexander III adopted Pobedonostev's creed of 'Autocracy, Orthodoxy and Nationality', which effectively meant **Russification** – the enforcing of Russian language on the culture of the other **ethnic minorities** in the empire.

- Russian was declared to be the official first language, so that trials and local government had to be conducted in Russian.
- Public office was closed to those who did not speak Russian fluently.
- Adherence to the Orthodox Church was encouraged. In the Baltic region, 37,000 Lutherans converted to Orthodoxy.
- Catholic monasteries were closed down. Members of non-Orthodox churches were not allowed to build new places of worship.
- Resistance to Russification was suppressed, often by the military.
- The nationalities that suffered most were the Poles, the Finns, the Baltic Germans and the Ukrainians.
- Russification was intended to 'unite' the country but it intensified national feeling among non-Russians and drove some to join opposition groups.

Anti-Semitism

The group that suffered most from Russification were the Jews. There were about 5 million, mostly living in western Russia.

- **Anti-Semitism** was ingrained in Russian society and, when anti-Jewish **pogroms** broke out in 1881–84, the authorities did little to curb the violence. Many Jews were raped or murdered and Jewish property in several cities was destroyed.
- Many laws were passed in Alexander's reign to restrict the rights and movement of Jews, who were forced to live in certain districts or ghettoes.
- Many Jews emigrated or were expelled and a number, such as **Leon Trotsky** and **Julius Martov**, were driven to join revolutionary groups.

How far do you agree?

Read the following interpretation on the reasons for Alexander III's repressive policies. Summarise the main arguments and then add your own knowledge to agree with or contradict each of the arguments.

EXTRACT A

Adapted from Martin Sixsmith, Russia: A 1,000-Year Chronicle of the Wild East *(2012)*

Alexander III wanted to unify the country by turning a Russian empire into a Russian nation, with a single nationality, a single language, religion and sovereign authority. His values were a return to (the old call for) Orthodoxy, Autocracy and Nationhood. Alexander had a pathological (extreme) fear of political opposition and was quick to declare emergency rule, suspend the law and restrict civil liberties introduced by his father. For a while, revolutionary activity was driven underground, but it never went away.

Comparing interpretations

With reference to the following two extracts and your understanding of the historical context, which extract do you find more convincing in relation to the policy of Russification?

Compare the arguments in the two extracts and use your contextual knowledge to decide which is more convincing.

- You could shade the sections of each extract that you agree with.
- Then, set out your answer, identifying agreements between the two extracts, and then disagreements, using your contextual knowledge.

Extract B argument(s)	Extract C argument(s)	Your contextual knowledge

EXTRACT B

Adapted from Orlando Figes, A People's Tragedy: The Russian Revolution 1891–1924 *(1996)*

There was nothing new in the policy of Russification. It had always been a central aim of the tsarist imperial philosophy to assimilate the non-Russian peoples into the Russian cultural and political system, to turn them into 'true Christians, loyal subjects, and good Russians'. As the regime's fears about nationalism grew, however, during the later nineteenth century, so its policies of Russification were gradually intensified. One cause of anxiety was that the Russians were losing their demographic domination as a result of the Empire's territorial expansion into Asia, especially, with its high birth-rates and overpopulation. The Slavophile nationalists, who were responsible for shaping the Russification campaigns of the last two tsars, argued that in this age of growing nationalism and imperial competition the Russian Empire would eventually break up unless something was done to preserve the cultural domination of the Russians. In short, they argued that Russian nationalism should be mobilised as a political force and consolidated at the heart of the tsarist ruling system as a counterweight to the centrifugal forces of the non-Russian nationalities.

EXTRACT C

Adapted from John Gooding, Rulers and Subjects: Government and People in Russia, 1801–1991 *(1996)*

Orthodoxy and Russian culture were now seen as vital to loyalty, and where they were missing disloyalty was assumed or at least suspected. Jews were treated as a particular problem. Rumours that 'the Jews' had killed the Tsar (one of the killers of Alexander II happened to be Jewish) triggered numerous 'pogroms' – assaults on Jews and their property – which the authorities did little to stop and may in some cases have connived in. With most other non-Russian groups, the government's aim was not so much to harass as to assimilate. Keeping their heads down was no longer enough; the non-Russians had to prove that they were reliable subjects by becoming Russian in faith and language. The government's belief that without cultural homogeneity the empire would sooner or later fall apart was no doubt correct, yet by its high-handed actions it merely stoked up the fires of nationalism and revolution and so brought nearer the very thing it wanted to avert.

Economic and social developments: industrial development and the land question

Economic reform under Mikhail von Reutern

Since Russia did not possess a wealthy middle class, **Mikhail von Reutern** (Minister of Finance, 1862–78) believed the government must direct economic change. Consequently, von Reutern introduced the following economic reforms:

- Tax-farming was abolished (companies could no longer buy the right to collect taxes).
- The Treasury was reformed and budgeting and auditing systems were established.
- Credit facilities were made available through the establishment of banks.
- Subsidies were offered to private railway companies and other industrial initiatives.
- Government-guaranteed annual dividends were provided for foreign investors.
- Tariffs on trade were lowered and trade treaties were negotiated.

Strengths of reforms	Limitations of reforms
• The cotton industry and mining both expanded. • There was some improvement in agriculture.	• Transport and labour mobility remained limited. • Growth was slow. • The Russian currency was unstable and much income went towards paying off debts.

Industrialisation under Ivan Vyshnegradsky

Despite some progress under Reutern, Russia still remained undeveloped in relation to Western Europe. **Ivan Vyshnegradsky** (Minister of Finance, 1887–92) tried to build up industry by increasing:

- **import tariffs** by as much as 30 per cent in order to boost home production
- grain exports by forcing peasants to sell grain to the state
- loans from abroad (e.g. from France, 1888).

Results

- Grain exports increased by 18 per cent (1881–91) and by 1892 the budget was in surplus.
- Peasants suffered from heavy taxation, high goods prices and grain requisitions.
- A famine (1891–92) following a bad harvest killed about 350,000 people and Vyshnegradsky was dismissed.

Sergei Witte (Finance Minister, 1892–1903)

Sergei Witte:

- sought additional loans from abroad
- increased investment in mining, oil and banking
- encouraged European experts to oversee industrial development and advise on planning
- achieved huge expansion of the railway network.

For the results of Witte's policies, see page 30.

Agriculture and the land issue

Emancipation brought little change in agricultural practice:

- because most peasants had too little land (averaging about 4 hectares) to become prosperous
- owing to high taxes, grain requisitioning, redemption payments and the traditional farming practices favoured by the mir elders.

The landowners

- The biggest landowners were mainly noblemen.
- Many landowners sold off some of their land to pay off debts.
- Some abandoned farming to set up businesses or enter the professions.

The peasants

- The richer, more successful peasants, the **kulaks**, bought up land, sometimes with loans from the Peasants' Land Bank.
- The kulaks employed poorer peasants to work on their land.
- The poorest peasants became landless labourers.
- Many peasants were found to be unfit for military service.
- The average life expectancy was about 28. In England, it was 45.

Summarise the arguments a

Read the following interpretation on the reasons for the impoverishment of the Russian peasantry. Summarise the main arguments, as opposed to the facts, and rephrase them in your own words.

EXTRACT A

Adapted from Orlando Figes, A People's Tragedy: The Russian Revolution 1891–1924 *(1996)*

There was a sharp rise in the rate of household partitions following the Emancipation. Between 1861 and 1884 over 40 per cent of all households were divided. Such partitions made little economic sense – the newly partitioned households, like the ones from which they had split, were left with much less livestock, tools and labour than before. Peasant poverty did not have much to do with the development of capitalism. The basic problem was that the peasantry's egalitarian customs gave them little incentive to produce anything other than babies. The birth-rate in Russia was nearly twice the European average during the second half of the nineteenth century. This resulted in a growing shortage of land. By the turn of the century seven per cent of the peasant households had no land at all. Russian peasant farming was much less intensive, with grain yields at barely half the level reached in the rest of Europe. Sowing, threshing and winnowing were all done by hand, long after they had been mechanized elsewhere.

 Support or challenge? a

Below is a sample A-level exam question that asks how far you agree with a specific statement. Following it is a list of factors which are relevant to the question. Using your own knowledge and information from the page opposite, decide whether these factors support or challenge the statement in the question.

'The basis for Russia's industrial growth was firmly laid in the years from 1855 to 1894.' Assess the validity of this view.

1 Grain exports were increased and, by 1892, the Russian budget was in surplus.

2 Russia's industrial development depended on foreign investment and expertise.

3 The peasants suffered from heavy taxation and high goods prices.

4 There was considerable growth in the cotton and mining industries.

5 Agricultural productivity remained far lower than in most of Europe.

6 The railway network was expanded.

Exam focus (AS-level)

Below is a sample Level 4 AS essay. Read it and the comments around it.

'Alexander II was a liberal reformer in the years 1855–81.' Explain why you agree or disagree with this view.

Alexander II can be seen as a liberal reformer largely because of the emancipation of the serfs. His military, legal, educational and other reforms also had a liberating effect for millions of Russians. However, some of these reforms contained elements that were restrictive while, from the late 1860s, Alexander resorted to repressive policies which further moderated the liberal element of his early reforms.

> This introduction is clearly focused on the question and highlights the line of argument to be followed, so that the structure of the essay is foreshadowed.

The 1861 emancipation of the serfs brought extensive freedoms to millions of peasants. They were now able to own their own property, to marry freely, to set up their own businesses and go to court. Above all, they could no longer be bought or sold. This reform provided, for some peasants, the opportunity for economic advancement, and many were able to farm profitably and buy more land, often from the nobility, in the years ahead. Furthermore, through the commune, or mir, the peasants were given responsibility for distributing the freed land and collecting taxes. Thus, it can be argued that Alexander deserves to be viewed as a liberal reformer for emancipation alone.

> Clear argument about the key event of the reign with plenty of precise, specific detail in support and reference back to the question in the concluding sentence.

However, there were significant defects, as far as the peasants were concerned, which limited the liberal aspects of emancipation. The peasants were saddled with huge redemption payments, to be paid over 49 years. They often received less, and worse, land than they had worked before. Furthermore, the communes could be highly restrictive. For instance, they were often unwilling to give permission to peasants who wished to leave because the commune as a whole would have to take on any redemption payments they left behind. Most communes continued to practise traditional, often restrictive, farming practices, such as distributing land in strips and dictating which crops would be grown. The more enterprising peasants were often thus prevented from taking economic initiatives and bettering themselves materially. It is not surprising that there were numerous outbreaks of peasant unrest in the 1860s given that many peasants felt that they had not been granted the freedoms they expected.

> This paragraph indicates the opposing argument concerning emancipation. The argument is well developed with a range of evidence.

Military reforms were significant in freeing the largely peasant army from the burden of 25-year periods of military service and the threat of corporal punishment, while much less use was to be made of capital punishment. The soldiers were provided with better medical care and all, not just peasants, were made liable to conscription, even if the monied could buy their way out. The millions who served in the army were undoubtedly freed from some of the harsher aspects of army life.

> This paragraph extends the range of the essay by introducing a second key factor – military reform – and its main point is well made.

Alexander's legal reforms made for a more open, fairer and less corrupt legal system. The judiciary were paid and thus were enabled to be more independent in their judgements and less prone to accepting bribes or being subjected to pressure from the authorities. Juries were to be used in criminal cases with barristers to represent the defendants. Those brought to court undoubtedly stood a better chance of receiving a fair trial.

> Another key factor – legal reforms – is addressed with precise, specific detail in support of the argument.

Alexander introduced elected, representative government at district and provincial levels although he did not concede the liberal intelligentsia's demand for a national body. The Zemstva were given responsibility for education, public health and the upkeep of roads. They provided enhanced employment opportunities for the professional middle classes – doctors, engineers, teachers – and many gained political experience from working in government. The Zemstva also provided a forum for debate on, and criticism of, government policies. However,

> Clear evidence is presented, both for and against the Zemstva, in relation to the question.

the Zemstva had no control over state or local taxes, while their presidents were invariably members of the nobility. Furthermore, Tsar-appointed provincial governors could overturn decisions made by the Zemstva.

Alexander's educational reforms contributed to his reputation as a liberal reformer. There was a huge increase in primary school provision and hence in literacy, while the universities were granted more freedom over appointments and the courses they taught. Censorship over newspapers and books was also eased. However, these and other reforms came under threat from the late 1860s, particularly after assassination attempts on the Tsar. Church control over primary schools was restored and universities were subject to far more interference. The scope of the Third Section was increased and, from 1878, political crimes were tried in secret in military courts.

In conclusion, emancipation and the wide-ranging reforms which followed were hugely liberating for millions of Russians, especially when compared to the past, even if many, particularly among the peasantry, were disappointed with the limitations of emancipation. The repressive policies of later years restricted the recently granted freedoms, particularly for the intelligentsia, but the vast majority of the population was certainly freer even if most were no better off in material terms. Thus, Alexander II deserves to be seen as a liberal reformer.

Specific, relevant detail about liberal aspects of educational reform, then a clear signpost of change to the opposing argument half way through in order to explain the nature of the repressive policies which curbed freedoms. However, this balancing section could be further developed to challenge the view that Alexander II was a liberal reformer.

This is a good conclusion with clear, balanced, well-supported judgement.

This is a good essay. It maintains a clear focus on the question. A wide range of factors is considered with precise, specific evidence in support of its arguments. It is clearly organised and effectively communicated. It demonstrates sound, balanced judgement, most notably in its concluding sentence. However, it omits to stress that Alexander remained an autocrat and this limited the extent of his liberal reform. Nevertheless, this is a high Level 4 essay.

What makes a good answer?

List the characteristics of a good essay, using the example and comments above.

Exam focus (A-level)

Below is a sample Level 5 essay. It was written in response to an A-level question. Read it and the comments around it.

How successful were the Tsarist governments in promoting economic modernisation in the years 1861–94?

In many respects, the Tsarist governments appear to have been extremely successful in promoting economic modernisation. Before 1861, Russia was among the most backward nations of Europe, both industrially and agriculturally, and was the last to retain a serf economy; by 1894, it was a fast-industrialising economy and its agriculture was being transformed as more wealthy kulak peasants were buying out the less successful former serfs and improving the land they farmed. The transformation in a short space of time certainly appeared impressive. In 1894, Russia's annual rate of growth was, at nearly ten per cent, higher than that of any other industrial country. Nevertheless, the statistics hide major problems within the economy and, in reality, economic modernisation had not been successfully achieved in Russia by 1894.

The emancipation of the serfs in 1861 began the process of economic modernisation by freeing labour from centuries-old constraints and permitting change in the towns and the countryside. The results were not immediate since former serfs were held back by the redemption dues they were required to pay and the control of the mir which collected these, but ultimately emancipation allowed greater mobility of labour, which is an essential feature of economic modernisation.

From the time of Alexander II, 'state capitalism' helped to transform the economy. This was practised by successive finance ministers – Reutern, Vyshnegradsky and Witte – who built up government finance to kick-start economic growth. Reutern successfully improved the collection and accounting of taxes (abolishing tax-farmers), extended credit facilities, gave government subsidies to businesses and encouraged foreign investment by offering government-guaranteed annual dividends. However, a third of all government expenditure was consumed by debt repayment so that the economy remained comparatively weak in the 1860s and 1870s. Nevertheless, by 1881, Russia had already taken the first steps towards economic modernisation, creating a new economic infrastructure.

Vyshnegradsky and Witte took economic modernisation a stage further and were successful in promoting not only the further spread of the railways but also the growth of heavy industry, which had previously been neglected. The largely state-owned railway system grew from 2,000 kilometres of track in 1860 to 30,000 by 1894. Huge industrial complexes were developed, including the Baku oilfields, while St Petersburg and Moscow were transformed into large industrial cities.

However, the Tsarist governments were not entirely successful in their quest for economic modernisation. Their achievements were largely won at the expense of the peasants, who were driven too hard to provide grain for sale abroad, particularly by Vyshnegradsky. The peasant famine of 1891–92 demonstrated the limitations of his policy and he was forced to resign. Nevertheless, Witte maintained a similar policy, oppressing the peasants with grain requisitions and high indirect taxation. This was not only socially ruinous; it also prevented improvement in agriculture and the growth of an internal market to stimulate industry.

The opening sentence offers one side of the picture while the final one states the candidate's own viewpoint. Between the two is an excellent overview of the period of the question. It shows awareness of dates and overall understanding.

Highlights the importance of emancipation as the start of modernisation.

This paragraph has much relevant detail, showing breadth of knowledge. The candidate has not been side-tracked into description. Instead, the examples of government intervention are used to support the opening comment that 'state capitalism' transformed the economy while recognising that progress was moderate in the early years.

Again, the knowledge and detail is impressive here.

The first sentence opens the way for the balancing argument: the ways in which the Tsarist governments were not successful.

Economic modernisation was also reliant on foreigners – for capital and for their managerial and technical expertise. It was the wealth of the Nobel and Rothschild families, for example, that lay behind the expansion at Baku, while reliance on foreign capital meant that 20 per cent of the budget was used to pay off foreign debt, ten times as much as was spent on education. Furthermore, the policy of unremitting industrialisation had caused huge social problems by 1894, with a discontented urban population living and working in often appalling and unregulated conditions. There was no state-run workers' insurance and it was illegal for workers to strike.

Moreover, the rural economy had failed to modernise to the same degree as industry. Although agriculture enjoyed a boom in the years immediately after emancipation, most farming remained small-scale. Population growth exacerbated the peasants' position. A small class of kulaks benefited from buying out their poorer neighbours with the help of loans from the government Peasant Land Bank, set up in 1885. However, for every peasant family that thrived, many more fell beneath the poverty line and became landless labourers.

Therefore, it would be fair to say that the Russian governments were only superficially successful in modernising the Russian economy in the years 1861 to 1894. They were hampered by their own disregard for the workforce – both urban and rural – and a narrow appreciation of what economic modernisation demanded. While the statistics might look impressive, Russia only grew so substantially because it started from a very low point. Some important steps had been taken, but there was a considerable distance to go, particularly in the development of agriculture, which still provided a livelihood for the vast majority of the population.

Shows very clearly and directly the deficiencies of Tsarist policies in industry, in financial and social terms.

This paragraph further develops the argument about limits of modernisation, specifically in agriculture.

This is a strong conclusion which repeats the view of the introduction and summarises the evidence on which that view has been based. It also pays due attention to the word 'modernise', showing that the question has been fully understood and addressed.

This is a very good answer. It responds explicitly to the words and dates of the question, offers plentiful comment backed by precise and detailed supporting information, balances success against failure in an analytical way and offers clear judgement. The view set out in the introduction is sustained through a series of well-structured and tightly focused paragraphs to provide a convincing response. Therefore the essay deserves a Level 5 mark.

Reverse engineering

The best essays are based on careful plans. Read this essay and the comments and try to work out the general points of the plan used to write this essay. Once you have done this, note down the specific examples used to support each general point.

2 The collapse of autocracy, 1894–1917

Political authority, government and Tsar: Nicholas II and the 1905 Revolution

REVISED

The personal rule of Nicholas II (1894–1917)

In September 1894, Alexander III died at the age of 49, leaving his 26-year-old son Nicholas as Emperor of Russia. **Nicholas II** admitted he had little idea of how to rule when he came to the throne. Nevertheless, he felt he had a God-given duty to fulfil. He was determined to rule 'as his father had done', yet he proved incapable of making firm decisions or providing any sense of direction. The new Tsar relied on the army and Okhrana to deal with challenges to his authority.

There was increasingly widespread unrest in both towns and the countryside as the Tsarist government appeared to offer no prospect of change. In 1903, the Tsar, who was easily influenced, dismissed his most competent adviser, Sergei Witte (see page 30), leaving himself surrounded by reactionary ministers. While peasants suffering from land hunger destroyed landlords' barns and seized woodland and pasture, industrial workers formed illegal **trade unions** and became involved in strikes. In St Petersburg in 1904, an official union, supported by the government, was formed by **Father Gapon**, in order to prevent workers joining the radical socialists.

War with Japan

- In January 1904, the Japanese attacked the Russian naval base at Port Arthur in the Far East.
- Plehve, the Minister for Internal Affairs, called for a 'short, swift victorious war' which would distract attention from political unrest at home.
- In March 1904, Russian forces were defeated at Mukden, with 90,000 Russians killed.
- In May 1904, 24 out of 27 ships of the Russian fleet were sunk in the Battle of Tsushima.
- In December 1904, Russia surrendered the naval base at Port Arthur.
- These defeats turned initial anti-Japanese patriotism into discontent and increased opposition to the government.

The 1905 Revolution: 'Bloody Sunday' and its results

Date	Event
3 January	Outbreak of a strike at the Putilov works in St Petersburg, which soon involved 150,000 workers.
9 January	Father Gapon led a peaceful march of about 20,000 workers to the Winter Palace, with a petition demanding improved working conditions and political reform. Troops fired on the marchers, leading to over a hundred deaths. Nicholas II later told the workers' representatives that they had been misguided and should return to work.
4 February	Grand Duke Sergei Alexandrovich, Nicholas's uncle and governor-general of Moscow, was assassinated.
March	An 'All-Russian Union of Railway Workers' was established and **soviets** of elected factory workers were formed to co-ordinate strikes.
June	Naval mutiny on the battleship *Potemkin*. In Odessa, the authorities tried to disperse sympathetic crowds, killing more than 2,000.
August	Peasants rioted and a 'Peasants' Union' was formed.
6 August	Nicholas promised a restricted State **Duma**, which revolutionaries regarded as too weak.
23 September	A printers' strike in Moscow spread to St Petersburg and other cities, creating a general strike in October.

! Simple essay style

Below is a sample exam question. Use your own knowledge and the information on the opposite page to produce a plan for this question. Choose four general points and provide three pieces of specific information to support each general point. Remember that there will be other, more long-term, reasons for the outbreak of the 1905 Revolution.

Once you have planned your essay, write the introduction and conclusion for the essay. The introduction should list the points to be discussed in the essay.

The conclusion should summarise the key points and justify which point was the most important.

'The outbreak of revolution in St Petersburg in 1905 was due to the incompetence of Tsar Nicholas II.' Explain why you agree or disagree with reference to the years 1894 to 1905.

i Introducing and concluding an argument

Read the A-level exam essay title below.

How good is the proposed introduction?

How effective is the proposed conclusion?

Could either be improved, especially to reach Level 5? (See page 7 for mark scheme.)

'The political unrest of 1905 was the result of failures in government policy since 1881.' Assess the validity of this view.

Introduction

There were both short-term and longer-term reasons for the political unrest of 1905. The immediate cause was the treatment of the marchers on Bloody Sunday in January 1905 and the Tsar's unsympathetic response. However, there were longer-term causes, such as the harsh, repressive nature of Tsarist rule in the time of Alexander III and the government's mishandling of the famine of 1891–2. Furthermore, some of the unrest was caused by factors that cannot be blamed directly on failures in government policy.

Conclusion

The incompetence of successive governments, whether in response to the Great Famine of 1891–2 or their conduct of the Japanese war in 1904 and the resulting discontent in 1905, was largely due to failures in government policy.

The October Manifesto and Duma government

The October Manifesto

By October 1905, Russia seemed near to collapse. There were strikes and demonstrations in the main cities and peasant uprisings in the countryside. The St Petersburg Soviet was set up to organise a general strike, which began in October. Under increasing pressure from his advisers, the Tsar issued a decree promising:

- civil liberties, such as freedom of speech, conscience, press and assembly for all
- a State Duma, elected by **universal suffrage**, to pass laws.

The impact of the Manifesto

- Most liberals, such as the '**Kadets**' (see page 36), Progressives and **Octobrists**, accepted the Manifesto.
- The Socialist Revolutionaries (SRs) and the SDs (see page 38) rejected it.
- Many workers were unconvinced by the Tsar's promises and continued to support the SRs and the SDs.
- Peasant risings continued, especially with hopes of land redistribution.

The recovery of Tsarist authority

- Most of the army remained loyal and helped to storm the headquarters of the Moscow and St Petersburg soviets in November/December 1905.
- Most of the leaders of the soviets were arrested and many were executed or exiled to Siberia.
- Troops restored order in the countryside and the government promised an end to redemption payments.
- The October Manifesto split the opposition. Peter Struve, a liberal, said: 'Thank God for the Tsar who has saved us from the people.'

The 'Fundamental Laws', April 1906

A new constitution was drawn up and political parties were legalised for the election, although the SRs and **Bolsheviks** (see page 38) refused to participate. Then, four days before the first Duma met, the Tsar issued the 'Fundamental Laws', in which he claimed his right to:

- exercise 'supreme autocratic power'
- initiate legislation and approve laws

- appoint and dismiss ministers
- summon and dissolve the Duma
- rule by decree in an emergency or when the Duma was not in session.

The Tsar never had any intention of becoming a '**constitutional monarch**'.

The Dumas

First Duma (May–June 1906)

- It was dominated by Kadets and radicals, with many peasant representatives.
- It demanded radical constitutional change.
- It passed a vote of 'no confidence' in the government and was dissolved.

Second Duma (February–June 1907)

- **Peter Stolypin**, the new Prime Minister, engineered elections to increase the number of Octobrists.
- However, the Bolsheviks and the SRs participated, increasing the number of radical deputies.
- It opposed most Tsarist proposals, including agrarian reform.
- It was dissolved and leading radicals were exiled.

Third Duma (November 1907–June 1912)

- Stolypin introduced an emergency law to reduce the representation of peasants and workers.
- Consequently, Octobrists and Conservatives dominated and the Duma was more compliant.
- However, there were still some disputes with the Tsar and it was twice suspended.

Fourth Duma (November 1912–17)

- The right- and left-wing deputies could not co-operate and the fourth Duma was increasingly ignored.
- It voted for **war credits** in 1914, but was suspended in 1915 after demanding more power.

Use own knowledge to support or contradict **a**

Below is an extract to read. Identify the main argument put forward to explain the failure of reform in the years from 1894 to 1914. Then, develop a counter-argument.

EXTRACT A

From Orlando Figes, A People's Tragedy: The Russian Revolution 1891–1924 *(1996)*

If there is a single, repetitive theme in the history of Russia during the last twenty years of the old regime, it is that of the need for reform and the failure of successive governments to achieve it in the face of the Tsar's opposition. Not that sweeping reforms would have been necessary: most of the liberals would have been satisfied by such moderate changes ... which would not have undermined the monarchy. But Nicholas was opposed to the idea of any limitation upon his autocratic prerogatives.

Comparing interpretations

With reference to the following two extracts and your understanding of the historical context, which extract provides the more convincing interpretation for the reasons for the eventual downfall of the Tsarist autocracy?

Compare the arguments in the two extracts and use your contextual knowledge to decide which is more convincing.

- You could shade the sections of each extract that you agree with.
- Then, set out your answer, identifying agreements between the two extracts, and then disagreements, using your contextual knowledge.

Extract B argument(s)	Extract C argument(s)	Your contextual knowledge

EXTRACT B

From Martin Sixsmith, Russia: A 1,000-Year Chronicle of the Wild East, *page 165 (2012)*

After the events of Bloody Sunday and the disaster of Tsushima, Nicholas was forced to rethink his unbending insistence on absolute autocracy. He offered concessions in the hope of defusing the building revolutionary tension. Had he taken such steps at the outset of his reign, he might have been successful. But now his concessions were perceived as a grudging response to irresistible pressure from the people, rather than the voluntary act of a reforming monarch. If the people could force the government to concede this much, many concluded, another push might bring the whole edifice crashing to the ground.

EXTRACT C

From Robert Service, A History of Modern Russia, *page 22 (1998)*

Nicholas would have made things easier for himself if he had allowed himself to be restrained constitutionally by the State Duma. Then the upper and middle classes, through their political parties, would have incurred the hostility that was aimed at the Emperor. Oppressive rule could have been removed at a stroke. The decadence and idiocy of Nicholas's court would have ceased to invite critical scrutiny; and by constitutionalising his position, he might even have saved his dynasty from destruction. As things stood, some kind of revolutionary clash was practically inevitable. Even the Octobrists were unsympathetic to their sovereign after his humiliation of Stolypin.

Economic developments to 1914: industrial and agricultural growth and change

The industrial transformation of Russia

Sergei Witte (see page 20) believed that industrialisation was essential to curb revolutionary unrest. Consequently the drive for growth continued and, from 1892 to 1914, the Russian economy grew at a rate of eight per cent per annum. Industrial growth was largely state-managed:

- Interest rates were raised to encourage foreign loans.
- A new rouble, backed by the value of gold, was issued in 1897 to increase business confidence.
- Foreign capital was raised to fund the development of railways, electricity plants, mining and oilfields.
- Heavy industry was prioritised over lighter industry.

The extent of growth

By 1914, Russia had 62,000 kilometres of railway track, the second longest in the world.

- The Trans-Siberian railway was built to link European Russia with the Far East.
- Railway development stimulated heavy industries, reduced transport costs for manufacturers and provided government revenue.
- However, the cost of industrialisation was high and Russia became dependent on foreign investment, which increased nearly tenfold from 1880 to 1900.
- By 1914, Russia was the fifth-largest industrial power.

The table below shows the huge growth in heavy industry from 1880 to 1910:

	1880	1890	1900	1910
Coal	3.2	5.9	16.1	25.4
Pig iron	0.42	0.89	2.66	3.0
Crude oil	0.5	3.9	10.2	12.1

Production in millions of metric tons

The development of agriculture

While Russia industrialised at a rapid rate from the 1890s, agriculture remained small-scale and inefficient. Stolypin, Minister of the Interior in 1906, believed that a radical reform of agriculture was required to prevent further peasant unrest. He wanted to increase individual peasant ownership so as to create a class of profit-orientated farmers, or kulaks, who would improve agriculture and, above all, support the regime.

- The mir system and collective ownership of land by families was abolished in November 1906.
- As promised in 1905, redemption payments were abolished in January 1907 and peasants became free to leave their villages.
- Peasants could apply for permission to consolidate scattered strips into single farms.
- A new Peasant Land Bank was established to fund purchases.
- Government subsidies to encourage settlement in Siberia were increased.

Successes of the legislation

- Peasant ownership of land increased from 20 per cent in 1905 to nearly 50 per cent in 1915.
- Grain production rose annually and, by 1909, Russia was the world's leading cereal exporter.
- Some peasants, the kulaks, consolidated their land, often 'buying out' poorer peasants to create more efficient and profitable peasant farms.
- Around 3.5 million peasants moved from over-populated areas to Siberia, creating a major agricultural region there for dairy and cereals.
- Some peasants sold out and moved to the towns to find work, so boosting the industrial labour supply.

Failures of the legislation

- By 1914 only around ten per cent of land had been transferred from communal to private ownership.
- In 1914, 90 per cent of peasant holdings were still based on scattered strips. Peasants were still reluctant to change farming methods.
- The poorer peasants lost their land and many became migrants looking for seasonal farm work or factory employment.
- Siberia proved difficult terrain for those who relocated there.
- Stolypin's reforms did not address the key issue – the redistribution of land held by the nobility, who retained 50 per cent of the land – and land hunger remained.

(i) Turning assertion into argument   a

Below is a sample A-level exam essay question and a series of assertions. Read the question and then add a justification to each of the assertions to turn it into a supported view, so creating an argument.

'Russian industry was transformed but agriculture changed little in the years from 1894 to 1914.' Assess the validity of this view.

Russian industry was transformed on the basis of an annual growth rate of eight per cent between 1894 and 1914.

_____

_____

The growth of the railways stimulated the growth of heavy industry.

_____

_____

Russia was industrialised with the aid of massive foreign investment.

_____

_____

Contrary to the view expressed in the question, Russian agriculture did change, especially as a result of Stolypin's reforms.

_____

_____

However, by 1914, nearly 90 per cent of peasant land was still held in communal ownership and based on traditional strips.

_____

_____

(i) Develop the detail   a

Below is a sample essay question and a paragraph written in answer to the question. The paragraph contains a limited amount of detail. Annotate the paragraph to add additional detail to it.

'Between 1894 and 1914, Russia became an economically strong and developed economy.' Explain why you agree or disagree with this view.

Between 1894 and 1914, Russia experienced massive industrial growth. By 1914, it had a huge railway network and had vastly increased its production of coal, iron and oil. Furthermore, agriculture became more efficient and profitable so that, by 1914, Russia had become the world's leading exporter of cereals. This shows that Russia became an economically strong and developed economy.

Social developments to 1914: the impact of industrialisation

While industrialisation helped to strengthen the Russian economy, it also brought a number of changes, some of which were to prove detrimental to the Tsarist regime. A new middle class and urban working class emerged.

The middle class

Factory and workshop owners, managers, traders and professionals (such as bankers, doctors and teachers) became more prominent in society and many played a major role in the Zemstva. However, the lack of an elected national assembly, at any rate until 1906, often made them opponents of the regime.

Urban growth and conditions

The urban population quadrupled from 7 to 28 million between 1867 and 1917, and by 1914 factory workers made up nearly ten per cent of the population. However, most suffered appalling working and living conditions and mortality rates were high. Some rented rooms in overcrowded blocks while others were housed in barrack-style factory accommodation where they ate in communal canteens and shared bath-houses. The least fortunate slept alongside their machines in the factories. Around 40 per cent of rented houses in St Petersburg had no running water and sewage was collected in handcarts.

There was limited regulation in the workplace, allowing employers to pay minimal wages which failed to keep pace with inflation. Women, who comprised a fifth of the workforce by 1914, were the lowest paid, and an industrial depression from 1900 to 1908 hit workers hard. Unions and strikes were officially banned before 1905, although some strikes took place illegally and were usually suppressed violently.

There was some improvement in the provision of education and in social welfare before 1914, as seen below, but every change led to demands for more.

Date	Law
1885	Night-time work for children and women was banned.
1886	Contracts of employment had to be drawn up.
1892	Employment of children under 12 and female labour in mines was banned.
1897	Working hours were reduced to 11.5 per day.
1903	Factory inspectorate was expanded.
1905	Trade unions were made legal.
1912	Sickness and accident insurance for workers was introduced.
1914	Normal factory hours were reduced to ten hours per day.

Industrial militancy

Real wages (what workers could buy with earnings) declined in the years 1910 to 1913 because of inflation and an employers' squeeze on wages in the face of growing world competition. Not surprisingly, there were numerous strikes in these years.

In 1912, the miners at the Lena goldfields in Siberia went on strike. They worked long hours for poor pay in a harsh climate and they demanded better pay and living conditions. Around 500 were killed when the army intervened. This was one of over 2,000 separate strikes across Russia in 1912. In 1913 there were 24,000 strikes and, in 1914, over a million. In July 1914, a general strike broke out in St Petersburg, but ended just before war began on 1 August.

Spot the mistake

Below is a sample A-level essay exam question and a paragraph written in answer to the question. Why does this paragraph not earn high praise? What is wrong with the focus of the answer in the paragraph?

'In 1914, Russia was stronger and more stable than it had been at any time since 1894.' To what extent do you agree with this view?

Russia may have been stronger in 1914 but it was certainly not more stable than it had been in 1894. In the last two years before war broke out, there was increasing discontent and a rash of strikes. Following the Lena goldfields strike, which was brutally crushed by the authorities, there were thousands of similar strikes across Russia and in 1914, there was a general strike in St Petersburg. This brought the Bolsheviks to prominence.

Complete the paragraph

Below is a sample AS-level exam essay question and the outline of a paragraph written in answer to the question. The paragraph begins with a relevant comment in relation to the question and ends with a further link. However, it lacks supporting examples. Complete the paragraph by providing some factual detail in the space provided.

'The economic changes of the years 1894–1914 improved the lives of the urban working class in Russia.' Explain why you agree or disagree with this view.

Although the economic changes of the years 1894–1914 brought some benefits to the lives of the urban working class in terms of regular employment and wages, overall the working classes in the industrial towns and cities suffered more than they benefited. For example ...

_____

_____

_____

_____

Consequently, although there was some improvement in the provision of education and in social welfare, the working classes saw few of the rewards of economic change.

Social divisions and cultural change

Living and working conditions in the countryside

Many peasants continued to live at subsistence level, subject to recurrent famine (e.g. 1891–92, 1898 and 1901). Grain output per acre was less than a third of that of Britain or Germany, yet peasants were driven hard to produce a surplus for export and pay high taxes. Rural population growth made conditions worse, particularly as holdings were divided between sons and the amount of land farmed by individual families declined.

The gulf between the richer peasants, the kulaks, who could afford to employ labour, and the poorest, landless peasants widened, and too few moved to the towns to ease the pressure on resources. Peasant mortality rates were high and very few had access to doctors.

Living standards varied from region to region. For instance, there was much prosperous, commercial farming in Ukraine and the Baltic provinces, whereas backward farming methods predominated in the noble-dominated areas of central Russia. These latter areas were to provide much of the Bolsheviks' strongest support.

The nobility and middle class

Although about a third of nobles' land was transferred to peasants and town dwellers between 1861 and the outbreak of war in 1914, the majority of the nobles retained their landed wealth while the Tsar relied on them to fill the top positions in government.

As industrialisation gained pace, so an emerging middle class of businessmen and professionals grew in size. A minority of nobles' sons also entered the world of industry and commerce, as did a number of enterprising peasants. Many of the middle classes served on the Zemstva.

The influence of the Church

- The Orthodox Church had close ties with the Tsarist regime. According to traditional belief, the Tsar ruled by 'divine right'.
- The Orthodox Church exercised considerable sway over the minds of the superstitious, ill-educated peasantry, which was of great benefit to the Tsarist regime.
- Priests had close ties to the village and were expected to read out Tsarist decrees and inform the police of subversive activity.
- The Church exercised censorship controls and Church courts handed down punishments for social and moral crimes.
- Under Alexander III, the Church was given increased control over primary education and it became an offence to convert from Orthodoxy to another faith.

Cultural changes

- The Orthodox Church had less hold over the growing working class in the cities, for many of whom socialist ideas had more appeal.
- Economic development from 1894 to 1914 brought new opportunities for women as educational provision was expanded.
- By 1914, 45 per cent of children aged between 8 and 11 were in primary school.
- By 1914, an increasing number of books were being published and the popular press flourished after censorship was ended in 1905.
- Cheap editions of the novels of Tolstoy and Dostoevsky were produced for the newly literate.
- By 1914, Russian culture had widened and embraced more than the elite.
- Nevertheless, millions remained highly respectful towards the autocracy and Orthodox Church and millions came out on to the streets of St Petersburg, Moscow and other cities on the 300th anniversary of the Romanov dynasty in 1913.

Use own knowledge to support or contradict

Below is an extract to read. Identify the main argument put forward to explain the position of the peasants in the late nineteenth century. Then, develop a counter-argument.

EXTRACT A

Adapted from Edward Acton, Russia – The Tsarist and Soviet Legacy *(1995)*

In the late nineteenth century, in addition to land purchased from the nobility [by the peasants], a vast amount of unused land was brought under cultivation, and the improvements in farming methods we have seen taking place in the 1860s and 1870s continued to bring a continued rise in yields. Peasants were also able to cushion the impact of indirect taxes by falling back on barter and home products when necessary, and the number finding non-agricultural work and remitting part of their wage to the village continued to increase. Recent research suggests that average grain consumption per head in the village rose during the period.

Developing an argument

Below is a sample A-level exam question, a list of key points to be made in the essay and a paragraph from the essay. Read the question, the plan and the sample paragraph. Rewrite the paragraph in order to develop an argument. Your paragraph should answer the question directly and set out the evidence that supports your argument. Crucially, it should develop an argument by setting out a general answer to the question and reasons that support this.

'There was little change in Russian society from 1894 to 1914.' Assess the validity of this view.

Key points:

- Urban growth and living conditions
- Working conditions and working-class militancy
- Traditional farming and rural poverty
- Deference to the Tsar and influence of the Orthodox Church
- Increased literacy.

Sample paragraph

The urban population grew, and factory workers made up ten per cent of the population by 1914. However, although some peasants migrated to the cities, most remained in the countryside. Because of the increasing population, the pressure on land intensified, yet most peasants became poorer. Nevertheless, they stayed loyal to the mir and maintained traditional farming practices so that Russian peasants were far less productive than their counterparts in other parts of Europe. They also remained loyal to the Tsar and the Church.

The growth of liberal opposition

Industrial and educational expansion produced a middle class seeking liberal change. Their main support came from lawyers, doctors, teachers, engineers and other professional groups. They were joined politically by more liberal members of the nobility. Liberal priorities were **civil rights** and a State Duma which would initiate and pass laws.

Zemstva

The liberals were strongly represented in the Zemstva. Many of them were professionals (often experts in education, health or law) who were highly critical of autocracy. Alexander III's introduction of Land Captains in 1889 to remove complaining Zemstva members and overrule Zemstva decisions only increased their opposition. Furthermore, the government's inability to co-ordinate famine relief (1891–92), which the Zemstva were left to provide, exemplified Tsarist incompetence. However, when the Zemstvo of Tver petitioned Nicholas II for a national Duma in 1895, this was dismissed as a 'senseless dream'. An attempted 'All-Zemstva Organisation' (1896) was also banned.

Other liberal critics

Liberal intellectuals, such as the author Leo Tolstoy, helped popularise the need for political change. Even S.V. Zubatov, the head of the Moscow Okhrana, favoured liberalisation and was given permission to legalise trade unions in 1900. His experiment was abandoned in 1903 when one union attempted to precipitate a general strike.

Liberal ideas and ideology

Frustrated liberals formed 'Beseda', the first organised liberal opposition group, in 1899. This merged with the Union of Liberation, founded by Peter Struve, in 1903. Struve had been a Marxist but he was opposed to violent revolution and he believed in constitutional government. Union members wished to see the Tsarist regime develop into a constitutional monarchy. Fifty banquets, attended by the liberal elite, were held over the winter of 1904 to spread the union's message.

The liberal opposition had limited political influence before 1905 but were mostly won over by the October Manifesto and the establishment of a Duma. They were largely represented by the Kadets (Constitutional Democrats) who favoured a constitutional monarchy with parliamentary government, full civil rights, the compulsory redistribution of the nobles' estates and the legal settlement of industrial disputes.

The Tsar and the liberals

The liberals tried to co-operate, through the Duma, with the Tsarist government but were frustrated by the increasing intransigence of the Tsar and his advisers. A number of Kadet leaders were arrested after the dissolution of the first Duma in 1906. Then, after dissolving the second Duma in 1907, the Tsarist government altered the franchise so that the electorate was reduced in size. The Tsar increasingly ignored or overruled the Dumas, resorting to emergency powers to pass the laws he wanted. There was little semblance of constitutional monarchy by 1914.

Support or challenge? **a**

Below is a sample A-level exam question which asks how far you agree with a specific statement. Following it is a list of factors which are relevant to the question. Using your own knowledge and information from the page opposite, decide whether these factors support or challenge the statement in the question.

'In the years from 1894 to 1914, the liberal opposition achieved little.' How far do you agree with this view?

1 The liberal opposition grew in size and became increasingly critical of the Tsarist autocracy from 1894 to 1914.

2 In 1895, the Tsar dismissed the idea of a national Duma as a 'senseless dream'.

3 The attempted All-Zemstva Organisation was banned in 1906.

4 The October Manifesto of 1905 promised the election of a national Duma by universal suffrage.

5 In the 'Fundamental Laws' of 1906, the Tsar showed that he had no intention of becoming a constitutional monarch.

6 The Tsar dissolved successive Dumas and increasingly ruled by decree.

 Eliminate irrelevance **a**

Below is an AS-level exam sample essay question and a paragraph written in answer to it. Read the paragraph and identify parts that are not directly relevant or helpful to the question. Draw a line through the information that is irrelevant and justify your deletions in the margin.

'Nicholas II's unwillingness to co-operate with the liberal opposition made Russia much less stable by 1914.' Explain why you agree or disagree with this view.

Early in his reign, Nicholas II dismissed the request for a State Duma as a 'senseless dream' and an attempted All-Zemstva Organisation was banned in 1896. This refusal to co-operate with the liberal opposition did not make Russia significantly less stable at the time. However, ten years later, the Tsar's intransigence did make Russia less stable. He appointed Stolypin, who suppressed rural unrest and forced the leaders of the St Petersburg Soviet into exile. His unwillingness to co-operate with the liberal opposition in the Dumas or consider even moderate reform made it much less likely that Russia would evolve peacefully into a constitutional monarchy. Instead, it made it far more likely, by 1914, that some kind of violent, revolutionary change would erupt in the years ahead.

Radical opposition

By 1894, after years of repression by Alexander III, the populist ideal of a peasant-based Russia seemed far off. However, the famine of 1891–92 led to a revival in the idea of rural socialism.

The Socialist Revolutionary Party

The **Socialist Revolutionary Party** (SRs) was established in 1901. It combined Marxism with the Populist belief in land redistribution. Viktor Chernov edited the party journal, *Revolutionary Russia*, and called on both peasants and urban workers to challenge autocracy. The SRs carried out 2,000 political assassinations from 1901 to 1905 and, in 1911, they assassinated Peter Stolypin. Over 2,000 SRs were executed.

The Social Democratic Workers' Party

Marxist ideas gained more support as industrialisation increased and the urban working class grew in size. In 1883, Plekhanov (see page 16) established the first Russian Marxist association, the 'Emancipation of Labour', in Geneva. It smuggled Marxist literature into Russia, encouraging urban workers to collaborate with the bourgeoisie in order to overthrow Tsardom. Plekhanov believed attempts to rouse the peasantry were futile. Marxism attracted an educated following, including Vladimir Ulyanov – known as **Lenin** – from 1901. Lenin had been attracted to Marxism when he was a St Petersburg law student. He met Plekhanov on a tour of Europe in 1895, but was arrested and exiled to Siberia until 1900.

The **Social Democratic Workers' Party** (SDs) was founded in 1898. Only nine delegates attended, but they wrote a manifesto and elected a three-man **Central Committee**, two of whom were immediately arrested. From exile in Switzerland, Lenin wrote for the party newspaper, *Iskra* ('The spark'), from 1902 and produced a pamphlet, *What is to be done?* In 1903, 51 delegates attended the second congress in Brussels, then London, but disagreements between Lenin and Martov, the co-editor of *Iskra*, split ranks. Lenin's followers became known as Bolsheviks (meaning 'majority') after winning a crucial vote, while Martov's followers were called **Mensheviks** ('minority'). Their differences can be seen below:

Lenin's followers	Martov's followers
Wanted a small, centrally controlled, highly disciplined party of professional revolutionaries who would lead the Revolution on behalf of the workers.	Wanted a democratic party that was open to all.
Refused to work with other parties and trade unions.	Was willing to co-operate with other parties and trade unions.
Believed the bourgeois and **proletarian** revolutions could occur simultaneously.	Believed that the workers should lead the revolution and that a proletarian revolution could only happen after the bourgeois revolution.

Both the SRs and SDs rejected the October Manifesto and called for a general strike organised by the St Petersburg Soviet in November 1905. However, after 1905, the radical opposition had no clear leader: Leon Trotsky, Chairman of the St Petersburg Soviet, was exiled to Siberia and Lenin, who only returned from exile in November, fled to Finland in December.

The government still feared opposition, especially from the trade unions, many of which were closed down. The government failed to pacify working-class discontent but the Tsarist autocracy was not in grave danger before 1914.

! Delete as applicable   a

Below is a sample AS-level exam essay question and a paragraph written in answer to this question. Read the paragraph and decide which option (in **bold**) is the most appropriate. Delete the less appropriate options and complete the paragraph by justifying your selection.

'In the years 1894 to 1914, opposition movements failed to weaken the power of the Tsarist regime.' Explain whether you agree or disagree.

> The demands of opposition movements were **a major threat/a fairly important threat/not a particularly major threat** to the Tsarist governments in the years 1881–1914. The liberal intelligentsia's desire for a constitutional monarchy **was very threatening to/was quite threatening to/did not weaken** the Tsarist autocracy. The aims of the radical opposition were highly revolutionary but, in practice, it was **very threatening/quite threatening/less of a threat**. This was because …

! Interpretation: content or argument?   a

Read the following interpretation on the appeal of Marxism and the two alternative answers to the question. Which answer focuses more on the content and which focuses more on the arguments of the interpretation? Explain your answer.

With reference to your understanding of the historical context, assess how convincing the arguments in this extract are in explaining the appeal of Marxism.

Answer 1

> This extract says that, from the 1890s, Marxism was popular, especially with young people, because it was new and it was bound to bring success. It would not fail like populism had done. Instead, so it says, Marxism promised to turn Russia into a free and modern society and the factory workers would be able to rise up and overthrow the employers and the government.

Answer 2

> This extract argues that, from the 1890s, Marxism appealed to young radicals because, after years of failure and self-doubt, it offered scientific proof that socialism worked and would inevitably succeed. It offered the assurance of victory for the urban workers, which populism had never done for the peasants, and it envisioned a society that would be just and free but also dynamic and industrialised. Furthermore, it argues that Marxism offered an explanation of the exploitation and alienation which the rapidly growing industrial workforce was experiencing in daily life and gave them the confidence to challenge both their employers and the Tsarist regime.

EXTRACT A

Adapted from Edward Acton, Russia – The Tsarist and Soviet Legacy *(1995)*

From the early 1890s Marxism caught on among young radicals with remarkable speed. Several factors contributed to the appeal of the new ideology. It provided answers to every conceivable question with an assurance and a seemingly impregnable logic which the populists of the 1870s had sought but never found. It guaranteed the ultimate victory of the revolution. After decades of failure and the deep self-doubt of the 1880s, its offer of scientific proof that socialism was inevitable exercised a powerful attraction. History was on the side of the proletariat. And the vision held out was of a Russia transformed from grinding poverty, ignorance and rural backwardness into a society that would not only be just and free but modern, dynamic, industrial. [Marx's] analysis made sense of the social changes overcoming the Empire. A factory proletariat was being formed and, as populist agitators had already discovered, the proletariat bore all the characteristics Marx had depicted – it was brutally exploited, profoundly alienated and capable of striking heavy blows against employers and government alike.

Political authority, opposition and the state of Russia in wartime, 1914–17

REVISED

Military defeats

Germany declared war on Russia on 19 July 1914. As the vast Russian army was assembled, a surge of patriotism swept the country. Strikes ceased and the Duma voted for war credits. An All-Russian Zemstvo Union for the Relief of Sick and Wounded Soldiers was created at the end of July, with **Prince Lvov** (a Kadet) as president, and in August, St Petersburg was renamed 'Petrograd' to sound less German. The country was divided into military zones, civilian authority was suspended and the sale of alcohol was forbidden.

Despite some initial successes on the Austrian front in August 1914, the invasion of East Prussia met strong German resistance and defeats were inflicted at:
- the Battle of Tannenburg (August 1914), which left 300,000 Russian soldiers dead or wounded
- the Battle of the Masurian Lakes (September 1914).

A massive Russian retreat began on both the German and Austrian fronts, and reports of inadequate clothing and footwear and a shortage of food and munitions (e.g. two rifles to every three soldiers) were published.

The political impact of the war, 1915–17

- The Zemstva resented their loss of authority when they were doing more for medical relief than the government.
- Local and national industries assumed responsibility for supplies in the absence of Tsarist action. This encouraged political ambitions.
- The Zemstva and Duma accused the government of incompetence, pointing for example to the futility of the alcohol ban as peasants brewed their own.
- In August 1915, Kadets, Octobrists and Progressives in the Duma formed the 'Progressive bloc', demanding a change of ministers and constitutional reform. They effectively demanded a constitutional monarchy in which the Tsar would genuinely share power. The Tsar suspended the Duma.

- On 23 August 1915, the Tsar took over as commander-in-chief of the armed forces despite his lack of military experience. Although the government mobilised about 15 million men between 1914 and 1917, it was unable to provide sufficient clothing or suitable weapons for them.
- Nicholas was held responsible for the failure of the Brusilov offensive (June–August 1916). A lack of trained officers and Russia's underdeveloped railway network contributed to the defeat, which sapped morale and provoked desertions.
- Tsarina **Alexandra** (a German and intensely unpopular) and **Rasputin** assumed much influence over government and political appointments in Nicholas' absence. Rumours spread that they were sabotaging the Russian war effort and confidence in the regime fell. Rodzianko (President of the fourth Duma, which reconvened in February 1916) warned Nicholas but he did not respond. Rasputin was assassinated by Prince Yusupov in December 1916.

The economic and social impact of the war

The war drained Russia. Costs rose from 1,500 million roubles in 1914 to 14,500 million by 1918, while production slumped as workers and peasants were conscripted to fight. Industrial capacity was lost as Poland and western Russia were overrun by the Germans and naval blockades ended Russia's Baltic and Black Sea trade. There were vital distribution inefficiencies, partly due to the inadequate railway system, which was disrupted by fuel shortages, but also because railways were prioritised for soldiers and military supplies, leaving food destined for civilians to rot in railway sidings.

Peasants made the situation worse by hoarding grain because there was nothing to buy, while workers suffered unemployment as non-military factories were forced to close due to lack of raw materials. Petrograd in particular, where there was a 300 per cent rise in the cost of living, saw an escalation of strikes.

① Summarise the arguments

a

Read the following interpretation on the reasons for increasing social tension during the war. Summarise the main arguments, as opposed to the facts, and rephrase them in your own words.

EXTRACT A

Adapted from Edward Acton, Russia – The Tsarist and Soviet Legacy, *page 146 (1995)*

Political developments during the war directly reflected mounting social tension. The Tsar remained as steadfastly opposed to reform as ever. This was not the mere whim of a stupid man. It corresponded closely to the views of the High Command, it suited the major industrialists perfectly, and it was energetically encouraged by many nobles; they urged the Tsar to resist making any concessions, be it to the Duma or the zemstvos which might allow central or local government to pass into hostile hands.

⚡ RAG – rate the timeline

Below is a sample exam question and a timeline. Read the question, study the timeline and, using three coloured pens, put a red, amber or green star next to the events to show:
- **Red:** Events and policies that have no relevance to the question
- **Amber:** Events and policies that have some significance to the question
- **Green:** Events and policies that are directly relevant to the question

'In 1914, the Tsarist regime was strong and stable. It was the First World War that led to its downfall.' Explain whether you agree or disagree with this statement. Answer with reference to the years 1894–1917.

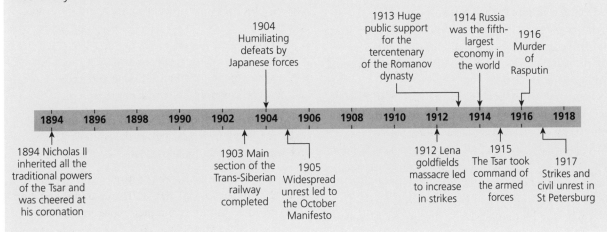

The collapse of Tsarist autocracy, February/March 1917, and the establishment of the Provisional Government

In Petrograd, in the winter of 1917, starvation and desperation produced a workers' revolution.

Timeline of the events of January–March, 1917

- 9 January: 150,000 workers demonstrated in Petrograd on the anniversary of Bloody Sunday.
- 14 February: 100,000 workers from 58 factories were on strike; the Duma demanded the abdication of the Tsar.
- 19 February: News that bread would be rationed from 1 March brought panic buying and some violence in bakers' queues.
- 22 February: 20,000 workers from Putilov Works went on strike.
- 23 February: A march of women on International Women's Day was swelled by striking workers and militant students, amounting to over 200,000 demonstrators calling for bread and reforms.
- 24–25 February: Demonstrations grew more menacing amid increasing calls for the overthrow of the Tsar.
- 26 February: Nicholas authorised the use of troops and ordered the closure of the Duma.
- 27 February: The Petrograd garrison mutinied, joining and arming the protesters. The Duma formed a Provisional Committee to take control. The Petrograd Soviet was created.
- 28 February: Nicholas II left his military headquarters to return to Petrograd but his train was diverted. His ministers were arrested on the authority of the Provisional Committee. The Petrograd Soviet issued 'Order No. 1'. This proclaimed Soviet authority over the army and encouraged the formation of soldiers' soviets. Sailors mutinied in **Kronstadt**.
- 1 March: The Duma and the Soviet agreed to support the creation of a Provisional Government.
- 2 March: Encouraged by his ministers and generals, the Tsar abdicated in favour of his brother, Grand Duke Mikhail.
- 3 March: Mikhail refused the throne, leaving the Provisional Government and Petrograd Soviet in charge. The Tsar, his family and most of his ministers were placed under house arrest. (The Tsar and his family were murdered by the Bolsheviks in July 1918.)

Russia and the Provisional Government

After the Tsar's abdication, Russia was left with two 'ruling' authorities: the Provisional Government and the Petrograd Soviet. The Soviet agreed to accept the Provisional Government's authority until a **constituent assembly** could be elected to draw up a new constitution. This arrangement was known as the **dual authority** or **dual power**.

- Prince Lvov became prime minister with a government comprising mainly liberal Octobrists and Kadets.
- **Alexander Kerensky**, who sat on the executive committee of the Petrograd Soviet, was the only socialist in the new government.
- The Petrograd Soviet mainly comprised radicals, especially SRs and Mensheviks, and acted as a 'guardian' of the rights of workers and soldiers.

Declining support for the Provisional Government

The Provisional Government promised and the Soviet accepted:
- civil liberties
- an amnesty for political prisoners
- the abolition of capital punishment and exile
- the appointment of independent judges.

However, the Provisional Government and the Soviet disagreed on many issues, e.g. on the conduct of the war and peasants' right to take over land.

The Provisional Government continued to fight the war, which led to mass public demonstrations and resignations of government ministers and their replacement by five socialists in May. Meanwhile, in the countryside peasants took the law into their own hands and seized land. In the cities, food supplies were chaotic, real wages fell and prices rose. By the summer of 1917, there was little support left for the Provisional Government.

How far do you agree?

Read the following interpretation on the reasons for the collapse of the Tsarist regime. Summarise the main arguments and then add your own knowledge to agree with or contradict each of the arguments.

EXTRACT A

Adapted from John Gooding, Rulers and Subjects: Government and People in Russia, 1801–1991 *(1996)*

The overthrow of tsarism was largely the work of the unguided and unorganised masses in a city where acute and massively worsening privation [hardship] created an irresistible groundswell of feeling that ordinary people would never have well being unless they destroyed this government and the existing social system.

The loathing ordinary Russians felt for 'them' went far back, as we know, but it had become more intense in the late nineteenth and the opening years of the twentieth century. What had saved the old order was that the tsar was untouched by this loathing, indeed was seen as a semi-divine protector of his people against the evils and injustices of life. Between 1905 and 1917, however, this immunity was finally destroyed. No longer a protector, the tsar crossed over in the popular perception to being the leader of 'them', the chief of the 'thieves'; and the sense of his betrayal was heightened by wartime rumours that he and his family were in league with the enemy.

Develop the detail

Below is a sample A-level exam question, followed by a series of statements to be used in an answer. Add relevant, specific detail to each of the statements in order to increase the value of the answer.

> To what extent was the collapse of the Tsarist regime in February 1917 brought about by the opposition of the Bolsheviks? Answer with reference to the years 1894 to 1917.

- Throughout his reign, Tsar Nicholas II refused to make genuine or lasting steps towards the establishment of a constitutional monarchy.
- In the First World War, shortages of food and equipment sapped the morale of the troops and contributed to military defeat.
- The Tsarist regime collapsed because Nicholas II's generals and ministers lost faith in him.
- Bolshevik propaganda turned increasing numbers of the St Petersburg garrison against the regime and their officers.

Lenin and the Bolshevik takeover, April–October 1917 REVISED

The April Theses

Lenin returned from exile in Switzerland in April 1917 and he gave a rousing speech, later published as the 'April Theses'. He demanded all power be given to the soviets, an end to the war and land for the peasants. In effect, he was accepting the peasant takeover of land and telling Russians what they wanted to hear. This helped to unite Bolsheviks under his leadership and, over the next few weeks, he managed to win over most of the Central Committee of the Bolshevik Party to his belief in non-co-operation with the Provisional Government.

The July days

In July, Lenin was joined by Trotsky, who had returned from exile in May. However, an armed uprising by soldiers, sailors and factory workers in Petrograd on 3–4 July, which attracted some Bolshevik followers, threatened to undermine Lenin's efforts. The Provisional Government used troops to break up the protest. Several prominent Bolsheviks were arrested. Trotsky was one, but Lenin managed to escape to Finland.

The Kornilov Affair

In July, Kerensky became prime minister and **General Lavr Kornilov** became commander-in-chief. Kornilov believed he could restore strong government and he prepared to bring loyal troops to Petrograd. Kerensky opposed Kornilov's 'coup' of 25–30 August and asked the Petrograd Soviet to help defend the city. Bolsheviks were given weapons and challenged the approaching army. Railway workers halted trains carrying troops to the capital and persuaded them to desert, while Kerensky had Kornilov arrested. The Kornilov Affair increased support for the Bolsheviks and weakened Kerensky's position.

Growth of the Bolsheviks

The Bolsheviks, who had refused any compromise with the increasingly unpopular Provisional Government, grew at the expense of the Mensheviks and the SRs, who urged national unity and therefore continued to work with the Provisional Government. In September, the Bolsheviks gained a majority on both the Moscow and Petrograd soviets, with Trotsky becoming chairman of the latter. By October, the Bolshevik Party had:

- a membership of 200,000
- a force of 10,000 **Red Guards**.

The Revolution of October 1917

From Finland, Lenin urged the seizure of power. However, the Bolshevik Central Committee was reluctant to lead an uprising against the Provisional Government without a **mandate** from an elected constituent assembly.

- 7 October: Lenin returned secretly to Petrograd. Kerensky, fearing uprisings, ordered the more radical army units to leave Petrograd.
- 9 October: The Petrograd Soviet set up a Military Revolutionary Committee under Trotsky. It claimed responsibility for the defence of Petrograd.
- 10 October: Lenin won a Central Committee vote for an 'armed uprising' to replace the Provisional Government with the Petrograd Soviet.
- 24–25 October: Around 8,000 Bolshevik Red Guards and Kronstadt sailors seized key positions in Petrograd (telephone exchanges, post offices, railway stations, state bank, bridges and power stations). Kerensky fled.
- 26 October: Red Guards and civilians broke into the Winter Palace and arrested the remaining members of the Provisional Government.

Comparing interpretations

With reference to the following two extracts and your understanding of the historical context, which extract provides the more convincing interpretation of the October Revolution of 1917?

Compare the arguments in the two extracts and use your contextual knowledge to decide which is more convincing.

● You could shade the sections of each extract that you agree with.

● Then, set out your answer, identifying agreements between the two extracts, and then disagreements, using your contextual knowledge.

Extract A argument(s)	Extract B argument(s)	Your contextual knowledge

EXTRACT A

The views of A. Berkman, summarised in Edward Acton, Rethinking the Russian Revolution *(1990)*

The revolution of 1917 was the product of popular revolt against oppression. It was accomplished 'not by a political party, but by the people themselves'. Time and again the self-proclaimed leaders of the revolution were taken by surprise by the initiative welling up from below – in January 1905, in February, April and July 1917. The masses were not enticed into revolt by superior leaders. Their extreme radicalism was not the product of manipulation or brainwashing by the Bolsheviks … The goals for which they strove were their own. They responded to only what fulfilled their own aspirations; the rest they rejected. In this sense not only February but the whole social upheaval of 1917 was 'spontaneous'.

EXTRACT B

Adapted from Richard Pipes, The Concise History of the Russian Revolution *(1995)*

In February 1917, Russia experienced a genuine revolution in that the disorders that brought down the tsarist regime … erupted spontaneously and the Provisional Government that assumed power gained immediate national acceptance. Neither held true of October 1917. The events that led to the overthrow of the Provisional Government were not spontaneous but carefully plotted and staged by a tightly organised conspiracy … October was a classic coup d'etat [seizure of power], the capture of government authority by a small band, carried out, in deference to the democratic professions of the age, with a show of mass participation, but with hardly any mass involvement.

Recommended reading

Below is a list of suggested further reading on this topic.

● Sheila Fitzpatrick, *The Russian Revolution* (1994)

● Robert Service, *The Russian Revolution, 1900–1927* (1986)

● Orlando Figes, *The People's Tragedy: The Russian Revolution, 1891–1924* (1996)

● Edward Acton, *Rethinking the Russian Revolution* (1990)

The Bolshevik government and the suppression of opposition

Consolidating the Revolution

On 25 October, Lenin had announced the seizure of power in the name of the All-Russian Congress of Soviets in the Petrograd Soviet. The next day, the Congress of Soviets met and socialists from other parties denounced the Bolshevik 'coup'. The Mensheviks and most of the SRs walked out, leaving the Bolsheviks and the more extreme left-wing SRs in control.

Lenin established a government of political **commissars**, called '**Sovnarkom**'. He was its chairman and Trotsky was Commissar for Foreign Affairs. Sovnarkom had the power to rule by decree without reference to the Soviet and it was made up exclusively of Bolsheviks. Several decrees were announced.

- The Decree on Peace called for an immediate end to the war.
- The Decree on Land declared all land to be the property of the people.
- The Decree on Workers' Control gave workers control of the factories.
- Ranks and titles were abolished.
- The banks were nationalised.
- Church lands were nationalised.

Suppressing the opposition

The early Bolshevik decrees were hugely popular, especially the Decree on Land, which helped to win over peasant support from the SRs. However, much of Russia remained outside Bolshevik control and many petitions, from factory committees and army units, called on the Bolsheviks to form a new government representing all of the socialist parties. Lenin, however, was set on one-party rule:

- Class warfare was encouraged with a propaganda campaign against *burzhui* (bourgeoisie).
- Anti-Bolshevik newspapers were closed down.
- Many civil servants were dismissed and replaced with Bolsheviks.
- The **Cheka**, the Bolshevik secret police, was established in December.
- Hundreds of Kadets, Mensheviks and right-wing SRs were arrested.

The Constituent Assembly

The main hope of the Bolsheviks' opponents centred on the elections to the Constituent Assembly. Lenin allowed the elections to go ahead because he knew there would be huge opposition if he did not. However, the SRs won most of the seats. Lenin was appalled and announced that an assembly made up of different political parties would be a bourgeois parliamentary democracy. The assembly met for one day, on 5 January 1918, and was then closed down. Lenin decided that the Bolsheviks would rule *on behalf* of the proletariat. Those demonstrating in favour of the assembly were dispersed by gunfire from Red Guards. There would not be another democratically elected body in Russia until after the collapse of Soviet communism 70 years later.

! Interpretation: content or argument? a

Read the following interpretation on the Bolsheviks' intentions and the two alternative answers to the question. Which answer focuses more on the content and which focuses more on the arguments of the interpretation? Explain your answer.

With reference to your understanding of the historical context, assess how convincing the arguments in this extract are in explaining the Bolsheviks' intentions.

Answer 1

This extract says that the Bolsheviks established one-party rule and that it was led by Lenin, who overrode other leading members of the party. Lenin had always wanted the Bolsheviks, not the soviets, to rule. However, it argues that the Bolsheviks did not mind if local soviets took power in the provinces as long as they were dominated by Bolsheviks.

Answer 2

This extract argues that, although one-party Bolshevik rule may have resulted from historical accident, it was always Lenin's intention to establish one-party rule and that he overrode other Bolshevik leaders. Furthermore, he did not even want to use the soviets as 'camouflage', instead preferring an 'unambiguously Bolshevik coup'. It concludes by stating that the Bolsheviks did not object to local soviets taking power as long as they were 'reliably Bolshevik'.

EXTRACT A

Adapted from Sheila Fitzpatrick, The Russian Revolution, *page 65 (1994)*

Some historians have suggested that the Bolsheviks' one-party rule emerged as a result of historical accident rather than intention. But if the intention in question is Lenin's, the argument seems dubious; and Lenin overrode the objections of other leading members of the party. In September and October, Lenin seems clearly to have wanted the Bolsheviks to take power, not the multi-party soviets. He did not even want to use the soviets as camouflage, but would apparently have preferred to stage an unambiguous Bolshevik coup. In the provinces, certainly, the immediate result of the October Revolution was that the soviets took power; and the local soviets were not always dominated by Bolsheviks ... It is perhaps fair to say that they had no objection in principle to the soviets exercising power at a local level, as long as the soviets were reliably Bolshevik.

i Introducing and concluding an argument a

Read the A-level exam essay title below. How good is the proposed introduction? How effective is the proposed conclusion? Could either be improved, especially to reach Level 5? (See mark scheme on page 7.)

'By the end of January 1918, Russia had a more autocratic government than it had had at any time since 1894.' Assess the validity of this view.

Introduction

Autocracy, meaning rule by one person governing from above, was a prominent characteristic of Russia by the end of January 1918 just as it had been in Tsarist Russia. Lenin was the pre-eminent Russian leader as the Tsar had been before 1917. However, whereas Nicholas II could claim to rule by divine or hereditary right, Lenin had no such justification. Both regimes made use of secret police, the Okhrana under Nicholas II and the Cheka established by Lenin, and both dissolved elected assemblies, the Duma after 1906 and the Constituent Assembly in January 1918.

Conclusion

In conclusion, in January 1918, Russia had just as autocratic a government as it had had under Tsar Nicholas II.

Exam focus (AS-level)

Below is a sample Level 5 answer on interpretations. It was written in response to an AS-style question.

With reference to these extracts (A and B) and your understanding of the historical context, which of these two extracts provides the more convincing interpretation of the effectiveness of the Tsarist regime in the reign of Nicholas II?

EXTRACT A

Adapted from J.A.S. Grenville, A World History of the Twentieth Century: Volume 1, Western Dominance, 1900–1945, *page 105 (1980)*

[In 1905] the loyalty of the army to the Tsar was never seriously in doubt, the soviets were dispersed, their leaders arrested, and gradually during 1906 in town and country the tide of revolution passed. With the need for compromise pressing, the Tsar soon showed his true colours. In the first Duma, a new party emerged, the Constitutional Democratic party, or Kadets as they were known. They were moderate and liberal and hoped on the basis of the October Manifesto to transform Russian autocracy into a genuine Western parliamentary constitutional government. Together with the moderate left, they outnumbered the revolutionary socialists. But the Tsar would have nothing to do with a Constitutional party. After the short second Duma, which saw a strengthening of the revolutionary socialists, the Tsar simply changed the electoral rules ensuring tame conservative majorities in the third and fourth Dumas. The opportunity of transforming Russia into a genuinely constitutional state by collaborating with moderate liberal opinion was spurned by the Tsar. As long as Nicholas II reigned, genuine constitutional change on the western model was blocked. Therein lies the lost opportunity to modernise and transform Russia.

EXTRACT B

Adapted from Robert Service, A History of Modern Russia, *page 21 (2003)*

[After 1905] the immediate danger to the regime had receded. The empire's subjects settled back into acceptance that the Okhrana and the armed forces were too strong to be challenged. Peasant disturbances were few. Stolypin had been ruthless ordering the execution of 2,796 peasant rebel leaders. The labour movement, too, was disrupted by police intervention. Strikes ceased for a while. But as the economy experienced an upturn and mass unemployment fell, workers regained their militant confidence. The recurrence of strikes and demonstrations [after 1912] was an index of the liability of the Tsarist political and economic order to intense strain. The Emperor, however, chose to strengthen his monarchical powers rather than seek a deal with the elected deputies in the State Duma. The Duma could be and was dispersed by him without consultation; electoral rules were redrawn on his orders. Opponents could be sentenced to exile without reference to the courts. There was little end to arbitrary [autocratic] government.

Both extracts are useful in throwing light on the effectiveness of the Tsarist regime, with Extract A being marginally more convincing in its explanation.

Extract A emphasises the loyalty of the army during the revolutionary disturbances of 1905 and explains the regime's effectiveness in dealing with the challenge to its authority posed by the soviets. Thus the 'tide of revolution passed' and the regime recovered its authority. However, according to the author, when compromise was urgently needed, the government proved to be intransigent in its attitude to the Dumas: the Tsar's government 'would have nothing to do with a constitutional party'. The extract does not deny the effectiveness of this policy. In fact, changing the electoral rules for the Duma produced 'tame conservative majorities' and, by implication, weakened opposition to the regime. The regime did not wish to be drawn into any kind of constitutional government. Without commenting directly on whether this stance made for more or less effective government, Extract A argues that the Tsar lost an opportunity to modernise and transform Russia, which would, arguably, have enhanced the effectiveness of the regime.

Extract B also argues that the regime recovered after 1905, that the armed forces and Okhrana were 'too strong to be challenged'. Furthermore, it argues that both peasant unrest and labour militancy were reduced as a result of action taken by Stolypin and the police, which is further evidence of the regime's effectiveness. However, the resilience of the Tsarist regime was severely tested by the revival of labour militancy from 1912. The Tsar's response was to resort to increased authoritarianism to weaken the Duma (also mentioned in Extract A) and send opponents into exile. The extract does not say whether such 'arbitrary government' made for a more or a less effective government.

Both extracts provide sound evidence to show how the Tsar neutralised the influence of the Duma. Extract B refers to the Tsar's refusal to 'deal with the elected deputies' but Extract A goes further and points out that the Tsar could have worked with the moderate parties and thus reduced the revolutionary threat to his regime. Extract A makes much of the Tsar's refusal to collaborate with the liberals in the Duma but fails to point out, as does Extract B, that the Kadets, the main liberal party, had themselves been very uncompromising in presenting the Tsar with radical proposals for reform in the first Duma. Arguably, compromise with the Kadets could have reduced the power of the Tsar so much that the effectiveness of his regime would have been weakened. Furthermore, Extract A does not point out how economic growth in the years immediately preceding the war led to increased worker militancy, or that the most militant political party, the Bolsheviks, wanted no compromise at all; in fact, they sought the overthrow of the Tsarist regime. Extract A does, however, highlight the 'lost opportunity' which, it implies, could have made for a more effective monarchy if it had been taken. Extract B, on the other hand, gives no clue as to whether the strengthening of 'monarchical powers' made for a more or a less effective regime in the years leading up to 1914. It simply states that it led to a continuation of 'arbitrary government'.

Neither extract explains what was the most important ingredient in an effective regime, particularly in one as autocratic as that of Tsarist Russia, which was the Tsar himself. Although he had not wanted to be Tsar, Nicholas II strove to be an autocrat like his father. However, he had few of the qualities needed. He was weak, constantly buffeted by his advisers and his wife, and many of those he chose to be ministers (although not Stolypin) were unfit to hold high office.

In conclusion, both extracts explain how the Tsarist regime recovered after 1905 yet proved intransigent and, by implication, lost potential support by refusing to work in partnership with the Duma. However, while Extract B seems neutral on the issue of how effective the regime was in its authoritarianism, Extract A is more convincing in its suggestion that the Tsar lost an opportunity to make Russia more modern and thus make his regime more effective.

This paragraph highlights a significant flaw which is common to both extracts.

The conclusion draws out two key strengths which both extracts have in common before explaining why one is more convincing.

This is a very good answer. It engages with the question and shows a good understanding of the interpretations. There is some sound comparative evaluation with wider contextual knowledge used to substantiate its judgements. This is a Level 5 response.

What makes a good interpretations answer?

Use this answer and the comments to make a bullet-pointed list of the characteristics of an A-grade interpretations answer. Use this list when planning and writing your own practice interpretation essays.

Exam focus (A-level)

Below is a sample Level 4 answer on interpretations. It was written in response to an A-level-style question.

> Using your understanding of the historical context, assess how convincing the arguments in these three extracts (A, B and C) are in relation to the political state of Russia in the reign of Nicholas II.

EXTRACT A

Adapted from J.A.S. Grenville, A World History of the Twentieth Century: Volume 1, Western Dominance, 1900–1945, *page 105 (1980)*

[In 1905] the loyalty of the army to the Tsar was never seriously in doubt, the soviets were dispersed, their leaders arrested, and gradually during 1906 in town and country the tide of revolution passed. With the need for compromise pressing, the Tsar soon showed his true colours. In the first Duma, a new party emerged, the Constitutional Democratic party, or Kadets as they were known. They were moderate and liberal and hoped on the basis of the October Manifesto to transform Russian autocracy into a genuine Western parliamentary constitutional government. Together with the moderate left, they outnumbered the revolutionary socialists. But the Tsar would have nothing to do with a Constitutional party. After the short second Duma, which saw a strengthening of the revolutionary socialists, the Tsar simply changed the electoral rules ensuring tame conservative majorities in the third and fourth Dumas. The opportunity of transforming Russia into a genuinely constitutional state by collaborating with moderate liberal opinion was spurned by the Tsar. As long as Nicholas II reigned, genuine constitutional change on the western model was blocked. Therein lies the lost opportunity to modernise and transform Russia.

EXTRACT B

Adapted from Robert Service, A History of Modern Russia, *page 21 (2003)*

[After 1905] the immediate danger to the regime had receded. The empire's subjects settled back into acceptance that the Okhrana and the armed forces were too strong to be challenged. Peasant disturbances were few. Stolypin had been ruthless ordering the execution of 2,796 peasant rebel leaders. The labour movement, too, was disrupted by police intervention. Strikes ceased for a while. But as the economy experienced an upturn and mass unemployment fell, workers regained their militant confidence. The recurrence of strikes and demonstrations [after 1912] was an index of the liability of the Tsarist political and economic order to intense strain. The Emperor, however, chose to strengthen his monarchical powers rather than seek a deal with the elected deputies in the State Duma. The Duma could be and was dispersed by him without consultation; electoral rules were redrawn on his orders. Opponents could be sentenced to exile without reference to the courts. There was little end to arbitrary [autocratic] government.

EXTRACT C

Adapted from Orlando Figes, A People's Tragedy: The Russian Revolution 1891–1924, *page 231 (1996)*

Once the revolutionary crisis of 1905–7 had passed, the monarchy no longer needed the protection of Stolypin, and increasingly detached itself from his government, paralysed its programme and began to pursue its own separate agenda, based increasingly after 1912 on the use of Russian nationalism to rally 'the loyal people' behind the throne. [Yet] by 1912, if not before, it had already become clear that no package of political reforms could ever resolve the profound social crisis that had caused the first crack in the system during 1905. True, for a while, largely as a result of government repressions, the labour movement subsided and showed signs of greater moderation. But in the two years after 1912 there was a dramatic increase in both the number of industrial strikes and in their level of militancy, culminating in July 1914 with a general strike in St Petersburg. The workers were moving over to the Bolsheviks, who encouraged direct workers' action and a violent struggle against the regime. Despite all the efforts at political reform, urban Russia on the eve of the First World War found itself on the brink of a new and potentially more violent revolution than the 'dress rehearsal' of 1905.

2 The collapse of autocracy, 1894–1917

AQA AS/A-level History Tsarist and Communist Russia 1855–1964   51

Extract A highlights the political recovery made by the Tsar's government after 1905. It recognises the importance of the army in restoring order and there is no hint that the armed forces were any less loyal or reliable by 1914. It bemoans the Tsar's unwillingness to co-operate with the moderate, liberal forces represented by the Kadets, and to turn Russia into a genuine 'Western parliamentary constitutional government'. The author accuses the Tsar of blocking reform and thus spurning the 'opportunity to modernise and transform Russia'. He refused to work with the Duma even after changes to the 'electoral rules' had produced a largely compliant body. The author clearly sees the Tsar as a negative, if not backward, force in Russia. This does not betoken any optimism in the political state of Russia in the years leading up to the First World War despite the public show of support for Tsarism in the tercentenary celebrations of 1913.

> The paragraph contains a well-supported elucidation of the main arguments of Extract A.

Extract B agrees that the threat to the Tsarist regime 'receded' after 1905: the 'Okhrana and the armed forces were too strong'. It identifies the role of Stolypin in crushing peasant unrest in the countryside. The author also acknowledges the effectiveness of the police in dealing with industrial unrest. The extract then refers to the vulnerability of the regime in the face of increased labour militancy after 1912 and comments on the resort to repression, for example with the use of 'exile without reference to the courts'. The extract also implies that the Tsar was high-handed and highly autocratic in his treatment of the Duma, dispersing its members at will and redrawing electoral rules. The author implies that these were retrograde steps: they signified 'little end to arbitrary government'. However, the author does not suggest that a strengthening of 'monarchical powers' made Russia any less stable or strong.

> This paragraph identifies the main arguments of Extract B very effectively and makes a discerning inference in the last sentence.

Extract C argues that the monarchy abandoned Stolypin and his reforming programme once the crisis of 1905–7 had passed and that the Tsar fell back on Russian nationalism to rally 'the loyal people' behind him. Certainly the Tsar relied increasingly on the Union of the Russian People and rejected any compromise with more moderate parties. Reliance on 'Autocracy, Nationalism and Orthodox' was highly divisive and, while it might rally a large body of ethnic Russians behind the regime, it would increase the feelings of alienation which Germans, Poles, Baltic peoples and Jews were already experiencing, thus weakening the empire.

> This paragraph focuses primarily on the argument about the use of Russian nationalism, with sound critical comment.

The author agrees that repressive policies were effective in reducing the instability threatened by the labour movement. He also believes that 'no package of political reform' could resolve what he sees as the 'profound social crisis' facing Russia. He believes that increased industrial militancy was such a severe threat to the regime, most evidently in the capital city, that Russia faced a genuinely revolutionary situation in 1914, one that made the events of 1905 look like a 'dress rehearsal'. The extract highlights the Bolsheviks' threat with their call for a 'violent struggle', presumably to overthrow the regime. Certainly Bolshevik slogans were widespread and, with increasing literacy and a burgeoning popular press, far more workers could read their pamphlets. Furthermore, Bolshevik activists instigated or directed many of the strikes in the two years following the Lena goldfields strike of 1912. Figes does, implicitly, acknowledge that the countryside was not as volatile, stating that it was in 'urban' Russia that a revolutionary situation was developing. However, even in St Petersburg, where the threat was greatest, the number of Bolshevik activists was still small and, across Russia as a whole in 1914, there were far more loyal, patriotic Russians – as suggested by the feelings towards the Tsar shown during the tercentenary celebration of 1913 and in response to the outbreak of war in 1914 – than there were revolutionaries.

> This paragraph makes effective use of wider contextual knowledge in order to make a critical evaluation of the arguments in Extract C.

None of the extracts makes any reference to the first ten years of Nicholas' reign. Most significant of all, however, none refers to what, it could be argued, was the greatest weakness of the Tsarist regime – the Tsar himself. In refusing any moves towards a constitutional monarchy and relying on the Okhrana to deal with any revolutionary threat, Nicholas II increasingly resorted to his powers as an autocrat. Yet he showed little of the decisiveness or strength of character required of an autocrat in his reign. He abandoned his ablest ministers, men like Witte and Stolypin, and appointed nonentities in their place, while the royal family's reliance on Rasputin damaged the Tsar's standing among his natural supporters, the nobility and army generals.

Highlights and explains a significant omission of all three extracts with supporting evidence from own knowledge.

This is a good answer. It shows good understanding of the interpretations and it elucidates the arguments of the extracts very effectively. However, the use of contextual knowledge to corroborate and challenge the interpretations is variable in its effectiveness: it could be used more fully in relation to Extracts A and B. This response would likely be awarded a Level 4.

Find the evidence

The most important element in analysing an argument is supporting evidence and examples. Read the answer again and identify where evidence has been used effectively to support a point.

3 The emergence of communist dictatorship, 1917–41

Lenin's Russia: ideology and change

In *State and Revolution*, which he wrote in 1917, Lenin had explained his ideology, specifically concerning the transition to socialism once the Bolsheviks had achieved power. However, circumstances, rather than ideology, largely determined policy in the early years of Bolshevik rule and thus the development of the Soviet state.

Initially, Lenin's hopes for democracy, following the Marxist view that government should be in the hands of 'the people', tallied with most Russians' belief that the main aim of revolution was to end all social privilege. The peasants, in their village soviets, which were effectively their village assemblies, divided up the nobles' land and shared it out. In the cities, the workers took control of the factories and responded eagerly to Lenin's call for 'the looting of the looters' and the confiscation of 'bourgeois' property. They made the wealthy share their houses and do manual labour.

Ideology and the end of the war

The creation of a socialist society in Russia was, in the minds of Lenin and Trotsky, dependent on a worldwide socialist revolution. This, they hoped, would emerge from the First World War as workers took on their employers and governments in civil war. This was particularly important as the Marxist idea of the 'dictatorship of the proletariat' was based on societies, like those in Germany and Britain, where the urban workers were the majority, not on one, as in Russia, where the peasants formed 80 per cent of the population.

However, the German military advance continued and the Bolsheviks, having promised peace to the Russians, were forced to sign an armistice. In his negotiations with the Germans, Trotsky played for time, hoping for revolution in the West, but Lenin insisted that Russia accept the Germans' peace terms in the Treaty of Brest-Litovsk. The terms were humiliating but Lenin took the pragmatic view that saving the revolution at home was more important than the spread of international revolution. This would provide the foundations for **Stalin's** later 'Socialism in One Country'.

Ideology and the one-party state

Lenin believed that the 'dictatorship of the proletariat' should be exercised by the Bolsheviks. He had no intention of sharing power with other socialists, as shown in his closing of the Constituent Assembly, and he increasingly bypassed the Petrograd Soviet. Rule by the Bolshevik-only Sovnarkom (the remaining SRs left in March 1918) meant that Russia became a one-party state. In March 1918, the Bolsheviks became the 'Communist Party'.

The Civil War (see page 56) had a huge impact on the development of the party and the state. It forced the government to adopt a more centralised system of government and to resort to terror to enforce its laws. Highly centralised government could, of course, be interpreted as fulfilling socialist goals. However, even when War Communism (see page 56) gave way to the New Economic Policy (see page 60) and allowed more capitalist practices, tight party unity was insisted on and Lenin issued a 'ban on factions'. Stalin later used this ban to defeat his rivals.

Many other features of Stalinist dictatorship were introduced in Lenin's time:
- The Church was persecuted.
- The powers of the secret police were extended.
- 'Show trials' were used to condemn the SRs.

Increasingly, decisions were made and policy shaped by two party bodies: the Central Committee and the **Politburo**. The latter had seven members and included Lenin, Trotsky and Stalin. In 1922, a new post of General Secretary was created to co-ordinate the work of the party. This post was filled by Stalin.

Mind map

Use the information on the page opposite to add detail to the spider diagram below to show the chief characteristics of Lenin's Russia.

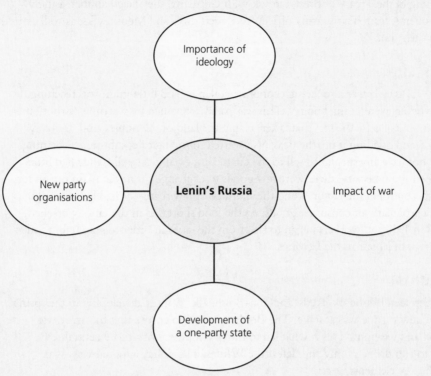

 Use own knowledge to support or contradict   **a**

Below is an extract to read. Identify the main argument put forward to explain the nature of the Bolshevik state. Then, develop a counter-argument.

Interpretation offered by the extract:

_____

_____

Counter-argument:

_____

_____

_____

_____

EXTRACT A

Adapted from D. Volkogonov, The Rise and Fall of the Soviet Empire, *page 69 (1999)*

Moscow became the capital of the 'revolutionary state' with the Bolshevik system which Lenin had created. It was a system that embodied Lenin's own personality. The Party was his creation and the state it governed was an expression of his mind and will. It is impossible to separate the history of one from the biography of the other.

Lenin and the consolidation of Bolshevik authority

The main problem the Bolsheviks faced in consolidating their authority was that they were a minority. They aspired to be a party of the people but they lacked mass support. Furthermore, following the signing of the Treaty of Brest-Litovsk with Germany, they faced an increasingly wide array of opponents, from Tsarist army officers to Kadets, SRs and Mensheviks, as well as foreign armies on their soil.

Economic crisis

By the spring of 1918, Russia was also facing economic collapse. Too little grain was reaching the cities so that the workers were going hungry. This was partly explained by wartime disruption of the transport system but also by the fact that, after seizing the land of the nobles (and, in many cases, of the kulaks) and dividing it up, the peasants reverted to small-scale, subsistence farming. Most of them did not have any surplus to sell to the cities. But, even if they did, they had little incentive to sell their grain because there were few goods to exchange for it: the main reason for this is that workers' control of the factories and the shortage of raw materials had led to a fall in industrial output, particularly of consumer goods. As the food shortages in the cities worsened, food riots erupted in 1918 and workers began to flee from the cities in order to search for food. This led to a shortage of labour in the factories.

War Communism

With a civil war between Bolshevik 'Reds' and non-Bolshevik 'Whites' developing in the spring, the survival of the new regime was at stake. The Bolsheviks had to ensure that the army was supplied with food and weapons. This is what led to the development of a more centralised system of control to run the economy and defeat the Whites. The policy adopted was 'War Communism'. The key elements were:

- Grain requisitioning: Red Guards and soldiers took grain from the peasants by force.
- All industry was placed under state control, with workers' committees replaced by managers reporting to government.
- Factory discipline was imposed, with fines for lateness and absence from work.
- Food rationing was introduced, with highest priority given to workers and Red Army soldiers and lowest to the bourgeoisie.

Necessity may have dictated this policy but it also enabled the Bolsheviks to extend class warfare and, in Lenin's words, to deal with 'class enemies'. The Bolsheviks saw centralised control as the way to develop socialism.

Red Terror

The most controversial aspect of early Bolshevik rule was the use of terror, which Lenin justified as necessary to ensure the survival of the regime. The main target was the peasantry. The peasants were to be forced to hand over grain to feed the soldiers and workers. The Cheka supported the grain requisitioning teams in seizing grain and thousands of peasants were arrested, imprisoned and executed, particularly in pro-White areas. So too were thousands deemed to be 'enemies of the people', whether SRs or other socialists opposed to the Bolsheviks, the wealthy, members of the clergy or independently minded workers. It is likely that up to half a million were executed between 1918 and 1921. Many more were sent to labour camps. The use of terror as a political weapon was further extended under Stalin but it was created under Lenin.

(i) Turning assertion into argument

Below is a sample A-level essay question and a series of assertions. Read the question and then add a justification to each of the assertions to turn it into a supported view, so creating an argument.

'By 1921, there were more similarities than differences between Tsarist autocracy and communist dictatorship.' Assess the validity of this view.

Both Nicholas II and Lenin depended on a political police, the Okhrana under the Tsar and the Cheka under the Bolsheviks, in order to instil fear.

_____

_____

Both Nicholas II and the Bolsheviks suppressed representative government, the former through the 'Fundamental Laws' and the latter with the closing of the Constituent Assembly.

_____

_____

The Tsar was seen as 'the father of his peoples', a kind of mystical figure, whereas Lenin deliberately avoided a personality cult in his lifetime.

_____

_____

Under Witte, industrial development had been directed by the state, but it was more closely controlled by the state under War Communism.

_____

_____

(i) Develop the detail

Below is a sample exam question, followed by a series of statements to be used in an answer. Add relevant, specific detail to each of the statements in order to increase the value of the answer.

'The Communist government faced similar difficulties, in the Civil War, to the Tsarist government in the First World War in feeding and equipping soldiers and workers, but responded very differently.' Assess the validity of this view.

- In the First World War, shortages of food and equipment were not overcome by the Tsarist government and this sapped the morale of the troops and caused disaffection among urban workers.
- In the Civil War, the Communists faced similar shortages but used force to extract grain from the peasants.
- The Communist government introduced rationing and ensured that troops and factory workers were fed.
- The Tsarist government tried to suppress popular discontent arising from food shortages in the capital.
- The Communists enforced strict discipline in the factories.

Stalin's rise to power and the establishment of dictatorship

REVISED

In December 1922, Lenin, partially paralysed after suffering a stroke, dictated his 'Testament', in which he gave his opinion of his fellow Politburo members. He was particularly critical of Stalin, who had insulted his wife, and suggested his removal from the post of General Secretary. However, other members of the Politburo were more afraid of Trotsky, the mastermind of the October Revolution and hero of the Civil War.

Trotsky	Stalin
Was charismatic, a brilliant orator and intellectual.	Was methodical and unspectacular, and seemed unthreatening.
Criticised the decline of internal party democracy, of genuine debate and discussion within the party, and the growth of bureaucracy with its tendency to make appointments on the basis of loyalty rather than merit.	As General Secretary, he appointed his own supporters to key positions. They then owed their place to him so that he could count on their support in party and government committees.
Was absent from Lenin's funeral because he was away recovering from illness and was misled about the date.	He delivered the oration at Lenin's funeral, praising Lenin as an almost god-like figure, and committing himself to carry on Lenin's work.
Believed in permanent revolution: as Russia only had a small working class, it needed the support of the working class in more industrialised countries. Therefore, Russia should actively work to encourage socialist revolution abroad.	Believed in Socialism in One Country: Russia could build a socialist state without external help. This had nationalistic appeal and allowed Stalin to accuse Trotsky of not having faith in the Russian people, even of being an enemy of the Soviet Union. Stalin reminded party members that Trotsky had been a Menshevik up to 1917.
Other Politburo members found Trotsky arrogant, aloof and dangerously ambitious. They feared he might become too dominant.	Stalin was politically astute yet others underestimated his political skill and ambition – until it was too late!

The establishment of the Stalinist dictatorship

Stalin's control of the party machine, and his ability to 'deliver the votes' in decisions made in the Central Committee or the Politburo, led to Trotsky being forced out of his position as Commissar for War in 1925. Two years later he was expelled from the party and, in 1929, he was deported.

Stalin maintained and extended Lenin's system of one-party rule and centralised control.

Stalin was particularly keen to assert his own personal dominance and meetings of party congresses were held less often. As General Secretary, Stalin controlled major appointments in the party and he developed a bureaucracy of loyal servants. He benefited from the huge increase in party membership in the 1920s and early 1930s. Most new members were younger and less well educated. They knew that loyalty could benefit them and their families. Most became reliable supporters of Stalin's dictatorship.

The 1936 Constitution

Stalin claimed that the new constitution of 1936 was 'the most democratic in the world'. It promised:
- considerable autonomy to the regions, but central government control ensured there was little
- elections every four years, but these were not contested. Only approved party members' names were on the ballot papers
- civil rights, such as free speech, but these were mostly ignored.

Some elements of the 'Stalinist dictatorship' were undoubtedly established by Lenin in the early 1920s. However, Stalin's rule was a personal one in which he was above the party.

Simple essay style

Below is a sample A-level exam question. Use your own knowledge and the information on the opposite page to produce a plan for this question. Choose four general points and provide three pieces of specific information to support each general point.

Once you have planned your essay, write the introduction and conclusion for the essay. The introduction should list the points to be discussed in the essay. The conclusion should summarise the key points and justify which point was the most important.

> To what extent did Lenin and Stalin exercise political authority in a similar way?

 Interpretation: content or argument? **a**

Read the following interpretation on Stalin's rise to power and the two alternative answers to the question.

Which answer focuses more on the content and which focuses more on the arguments of the interpretation? Explain your answer.

> With reference to your understanding of the historical context, assess how convincing the arguments in this extract are in explaining Stalin's rise to power.

Answer 1

This extract says that Stalin had the reputation of an unprincipled bureaucrat but that he was also decisive, competent, confident and ambitious, just like a leader. He knew he was not a good orator like his rivals and that they were not impressed by him, but he was proud of his practical nature and was determined to scatter and tear them up.

Answer 2

This extract argues that, although Stalin gained the reputation of an unprincipled bureaucrat, he also possessed the qualities required of a leader. Furthermore, the members of the Central Committee recognised this and that was why they chose him to 'lead the charge against Trotsky'. It implies that he resented his rivals' oratorical skills but believed that practical men were the 'party's backbone' and that his rivals would respect him, as they had Lenin, if he scattered his opponents. He would earn even more respect, even fear, if he destroyed them completely as well.

EXTRACT A

Adapted from Robert Service, Stalin: A Biography, *page 228 (2004)*

Stalin gained the reputation of an unprincipled bureaucrat. He revelled in his deviousness when talking to his associates. But there was much more to him. He had the potential of a true leader. He was decisive, competent, confident and ambitious. The choice of him rather than Zinoviev or Kamenev to head the charge against Trotsky at the Thirteenth Party Conference showed this was beginning to be understood by other Central Committee members. He was coming out of the shadows ... Stalin was tired of seeing his rivals strutting on the public stage. He accepted that they were good orators and that he would never match them in this. Yet he was proud that his contribution to Bolshevism was mainly practical in nature; he thought practical men like himself were the party's backbone. The practical men looked up to Lenin as the eagle who scattered his opponents like mere chickens. Stalin seemed unimpressive to those who did not know him and indeed to many who did; but he was already determined to fly into history as the party's second eagle. He did not just scatter his rivals for the succession: whenever possible, he swooped down and tore them to bits.

Economic developments: from War Communism to the Five-Year Plans

REVISED

Lenin said that 'Soviets plus electrification equals communism'. He knew Russia had to modernise in order to show that communism worked. In 1917 he had abolished private ownership of land and recognised workers' control of factories, effectively legitimising what was already happening in the countryside and cities. However, he knew increased state intervention was necessary because:

- The workers did not have the skill or experience to run the factories and production fell.
- With fewer industrial goods for sale, the peasants hoarded their grain as there was little to buy if they sold it.
- It was necessary to feed the workers and soldiers and thus win the Civil War.

Thus began War Communism (see page 56). In the drive to extract more grain from the peasants, the kulaks, in particular, were targeted by the requisitioning squads. The kulaks produced more food and were seen as 'class enemies'. In the cities, the factories were nationalised, working hours were extended and internal passports were issued to stop the workers leaving the cities in search of food.

The origins of the New Economic Policy

The Bolsheviks won the Civil War but failed to increase factory production. By 1921, industrial output was only 20 per cent of what it had been in 1914. In the countryside, peasants resisted food requisitioning, growing less grain rather than handing it over. Many killed their livestock to survive. Famine, disease and strikes spread across the Soviet Union (as the new communist state became known in 1922). Millions died. There were widespread peasant revolts and, most alarming of all for the government, an uprising in 1921 among the Kronstadt sailors ('the pride and glory of the Russian Revolution', according to Trotsky). The revolt was crushed but Lenin was shaken. In August 1921, he announced the New Economic Policy (NEP):

- There was an end to grain requisitioning. Peasants were to hand over 20 per cent of their grain (a form of tax) to the government but could sell any remaining surplus.
- The state would continue to control the 'commanding heights' of the economy, e.g. the railways, coal, iron and steel.
- Small businesses and private trade were allowed.

Results of the New Economic Policy

- Economic recovery was led by an increase in the supply of grain and other foodstuff to cities.
- There was an end to revolts and civil unrest.
- There was a revival of the kulak class of peasants and emergence of 'NEPmen', traders and speculators.
- However, industrial production was slow to recover so that peasants began to hold back their grain as there were few consumer goods to buy.
- Grain procured by the government by the end of 1927 was 75 per cent of what it had been in 1926.
- Stalin ordered grain seizures and decided the solution to the grain crisis was to develop 'large-scale farms of a collective type'. The 'battle for grain' had begun.

The Five-Year Plans

In December 1927, Stalin announced the start of a 'Five-Year Plan'. He had decided that the Soviet Union had to modernise to catch up with the industrially advanced states of Europe and the USA: 'Either we do it or we shall be crushed'. The Soviet Union would become self-sufficient and defend itself by building industries. To do this, it would export grain to pay for the machinery and expertise it needed from abroad. It would build Socialism in One Country.

A-level interpretation question

Below is an A-level exam-style question. Read the extracts and then plan an answer for each one of them.

Using your understanding of the historical context, assess how convincing the arguments in these three extracts are in relation to the aims and methods of implementing economic policy from 1917 to 1941.

EXTRACT A

From Orlando Figes, A People's Tragedy: The Russian Revolution 1891–1924, *page 770 (1996)*

As Lenin saw it, the NEP was more than a temporary concession to the market in order to get the country back on its feet. It was a fundamental if rather ill-formulated attempt to redefine the role of socialism in a backward peasant economy where, largely as a result of his own party's coup d'etat in 1917, the 'bourgeois revolution' had not been completed. Only 'in countries of developed capitalism' was it possible to make an 'immediate transition to socialism', Lenin had told the Tenth party congress. Soviet Russia was thus confronted with the task of 'building communism with bourgeois hands', of basing socialism on the market. Lenin remained full of doubts: at times he expressed fears that the regime would be drowned in a sea of petty peasant capitalism. But in the main he saw the market – regulated by the state and gradually socialised through co-operatives – as the only way to socialism. Whereas the Bolsheviks had up to now lived by the slogan 'the less market, the more socialism', Lenin was moving towards the slogan 'the more market, the more socialism'.

EXTRACT B

Adapted from J. P. Nettl, The Soviet Achievement, *page 119 (1967)*

The year 1928 witnessed the first of the Five-Year Plans. To achieve the required growth of industry, four basic conditions had to be met. First, the availability of natural resources. Here the Soviet Union was abundantly supplied. Secondly, a population structure producing a relative surplus in the crucial category between 20 and 45 years was required. This existed in the USSR. The other two conditions were more directly controllable. Extra food would have to be available to support the growing population in the industrial towns, largely made up of peasants moving from the land to form the new labour force. And the final condition was the formation of extra capital for investment. Without surplus agricultural supplies and capital for investment, no major efforts at industrialisation could succeed. Alternatively, surpluses had to be created artificially by squeezing consumption. In the Soviet Union, there were no obvious surpluses or spare capacity on any large scale. Nonetheless, with the vast majority of the population living on the land, a food surplus could conceivably be squeezed out by force – providing that the same peasant, viewed as a consumer, could be forced to make do with far less. In the vast majority of kolkhozy those who produced the food often did not have enough to eat, especially when the harvest was average or less.

EXTRACT C

Adapted from Edward Acton, Russia – The Tsarist and Soviet Legacy, *page 211 (1995)*

By 1941 the Soviet Union had established a mighty, if crude, industrial base. There were three key ingredients in this achievement. The first was an extremely high rate of investment. The millions of workers digging, carrying, building and assembling machinery had to be fed, housed and clothed. In addition the machinery being installed in factories and mines had to be paid for. During the early years the great bulk of it had to be imported from the West. The second ingredient was the massive mobilisation of underused labour. In little over a decade the industrial labour force rose from one-eighth to one-third of the working population. The third ingredient was the vast expansion in the scope of state power. Private enterprise was virtually eliminated.

The means by which investment and labour were mobilised and the entire economy brought under state control involved the use of force – force on a scale which beggars the imagination: whole social groups were brutally coerced and individual security undermined. The NKVD was involved in each facet of the industrialisation drive – the collectivisation of the peasantry, the enforcement of labour discipline, the supervision of industrial management. It oversaw a sprawling penal system.

Economic developments: industrialisation and collectivisation

REVISED

Industrialisation

The Five-Year Plans set high targets for each industry, which were then broken down for regions and specific factories. Failure to meet targets could lead to arrest, prison or worse. This led to pressure to put quantity before quality and to enhance the production figures. Massive propaganda campaigns portrayed the plans as part of the revolutionary struggle to achieve the final overthrow of capitalism and make the Soviet Union into a great industrial power.

The emphasis in all of the first three plans was on heavy industry – coal, iron and steel, oil, machinery – and electricity. In 1929, the targets for 1932 were revised upwards. None of these hugely ambitious targets were met but big increases in production were achieved (see table below). Electricity output trebled by 1932.

Product (in millions of tons)	1927–28 production	Target for 1932	Amended target for 1932	1932 actual production
Coal	35	75	95–105	64
Oil	11.7	21.7	40–55	21.4
Iron ore	6.7	20.2	24–32	12.1
Pig iron	3.2	10	15–16	6.2

Huge growth was maintained throughout the 1930s. Consumer goods were neglected, while rearmament was prioritised as fear of war increased in the late 1930s. Some developments were spectacular: the building of a huge industrial complex at Magnitogorsk within a few years and the construction of Dnieprostroi Dam, which increased Soviet electricity production by five times when it was completed. Many projects were achieved at huge cost to human life, mostly that of displaced peasants (see below). Living conditions for Soviet workers deteriorated, especially with the marked increase in the urban population. However, Stalin achieved his primary aim of making the Soviet Union into an industrial power that was, eventually, able to defeat Nazi Germany in the Second World War.

The Five-Year Plans

First FYP	1928–32
Second FYP	1933–37
Third FYP	1938–41
Fourth FYP	1946–50
Fifth FYP	1951–55
Sixth FYP	1956–60
Seventh FYP	1959–65

Collectivisation

Main features	Results
• The amalgamation of several villages into collective farms, with all equipment and livestock pooled • The procurement of grain to feed the expanding industrial workforce and pay for imports of industrial equipment • Thousands of party activists, backed up by soldiers and secret police, implemented the policy of forced collectivisation • The destruction of the kulaks in order to force the peasantry into submission • Increase in control over the peasantry by the state, classifying all who opposed collectivisation as 'kulaks' • By March 1930, over half the peasants had been collectivised (and 90 per cent by 1939).	• Massive opposition, e.g. burning crops and killing livestock rather than hand them over • Many collectives were run inefficiently by managers who knew little of farming • Decline in food production, although state procurement and exports of grain increased • Famine in Ukraine in 1932–33, leading to over 3 million deaths • The Soviet Union did not recover pre-war levels of grain production until 1939 • Millions were driven off the land, many into forced labour camps, to build the new industrial Soviet Union • Stalin achieved his aim of feeding the industrial workforce and exporting grain • Destruction of traditional peasant way of life, based on the family farm, the commune and the Church.

RAG – rate the interpretation

Read the following extract on the aims and impact of collectivisation.

Shade the sections you agree with in green.

Shade anything you disagree with in red.

Shade anything you partly agree/disagree with in amber.

EXTRACT A

Adapted from O. Figes, Revolutionary Russia, 1891–1991, *page 154 (2014)*

Stalin's war against the 'kulaks' had little to do with economic considerations – and everything to do with eliminating the defenders of the peasant way of life. Large collective farms amalgamated land from several villages. Many of the smaller settlements and their churches were abandoned or destroyed. The peasants were turned into agricultural workers in kolkhoz brigades. Tied to the collective farm by an internal passport system, the peasants thought of collectivisation as a 'second serfdom'. The collective farms were a dismal failure. They never really worked. But Stalin's aims had been achieved: the independent peasantry had been eliminated as an obstacle to the revolution's progress.

Introducing and concluding an argument

Read the essay title below.

How good is the proposed introduction?

How effective is the proposed conclusion?

Could either be improved, especially to reach Level 5? (See page 7 for mark scheme.)

'Between 1917 and 1941, the economy of the Soviet Union was transformed.' Assess the validity of this view.

Introduction

The commanding heights of the economy (coal, iron and steel, railways, etc.) were put under state control after the October Revolution and remained so throughout the period. Agriculture, however, remained under private, peasant control until the period of collectivisation, starting in the late 1920s, which saw over 90 per cent of farms come under the control of the *khoklhoz* by 1941. The period 1928–41 witnessed a similar transformation in industry, with the production of coal, iron and electricity increasing four- or five-fold by the time the Soviet Union went to war in 1941.

Conclusion

In conclusion, by 1941, the Soviet Union had become far more industrialised, particularly in heavy industry and the production of armaments, although light industry, and consumer goods in particular, experienced less development. The standard of living of most Soviet citizens improved little, if at all.

Social developments: class, women and young people

Class

In their determination to create a classless society, the Soviet regime encouraged communal living, with families sharing kitchens and toilets. Private life was subjected to public scrutiny, with the interests of the community seen as superior to those of the individual, especially the *burzhui*, the class enemy. However, the attempt to abolish private life led many to hide behind a mask of conformity in order to preserve their own identity. This is one reason why the leadership was so keen to unmask potential enemies in the **purges** (see page 68).

The October Revolution was intended to bring about greater equality and, at first, the workers and peasants took control of the factories and farms. However, harsh labour discipline was introduced under War Communism. Working conditions worsened under Stalin with the imposition of a seven-day working week and longer working hours. Then, in the 1930s, bonuses and payment by results were introduced to increase productivity, while the **Stakhanovite** movement further contributed to the emergence of a labour elite with higher pay and better housing. Living conditions in the countryside deteriorated dramatically during collectivisation, while overcrowding and poor sanitation characterised urban living.

Women

The Communist Revolution promised greater opportunities for women, such as access to a job and help with child care. Divorce was made easier and abortion legalised. Women began to work in increasing numbers and more nurseries were provided. However, women continued to do most of the housework, while divorces were mostly initiated by men. Then, with a falling birth rate in the early 1930s, Stalin began to extol the traditional family: Soviet propaganda portrayed him as a father figure and, increasingly, women as mothers rather than as workers. Divorce was made more difficult and financial incentives were offered for large families. Nevertheless, 43 per cent of the industrial workforce was made up of women in 1940.

Young people

Education was seen as crucial in building a new socialist society. From Lenin's time, free schooling was provided for all. It combined maths, science, Russian language and literature with vocational training and 'socially useful labour' in order to develop the skills needed in a modern, industrial society. Furthermore, universities and schools had a vital role to play in indoctrinating the young in a new, collective way of life. For instance, students were encouraged to inform on teachers (and parents) holding 'anti-Soviet' views. Nevertheless, undoubted educational improvements were made and, by 1941, about 90 per cent of those under the age of 50 were literate.

A youth division of the Communist Party, later renamed **Komsomol**, was formed in 1918 and a junior section, the Pioneers, was established in 1922. All Pioneers took an oath to the Communist Party and wore a special uniform. Komsomol encouraged its members to assist the police, do voluntary social work and set up political clubs in order to instil socialist values. Membership could ease educational advancement and enhance job opportunities. By 1940, Komsomol had 10 million members but not all young people became involved: some preferred Western films, fashion and music, which were frowned on by the regime.

Summarise the arguments

Read the following extract on the reasons for the change in Soviet family policy. Summarise the main arguments, as opposed to the facts, and rephrase them in your own words.

EXTRACT A

Adapted from O. Figes, Revolutionary Russia, 1891–1991, *page 183 (2014)*

From the mid-1930s a series of decrees aimed to strengthen the Soviet family: the divorce laws were tightened; fees for divorce were raised substantially; homosexuality and abortion were outlawed. Marriage certificates were issued on high-quality paper instead of on the wrapping paper used before. This dramatic policy reversal was partly a reaction to the demographic and social disaster of 1928-32: millions had died in the famine; the birthrate had dropped, posing a threat to the country's military strength; divorce had increased. The Soviet regime needed stable families to sustain the rates of population growth its military needed to compete with the other totalitarian regimes, which heavily supported the patriarchal family in their 'battles for births'. But the Soviet turnaround was also a response to the 'bourgeois' aspirations of Stalin's new industrial and political elites, most of whom had risen only recently from the peasantry or the working class.

Use own knowledge to support or contradict

Below is an extract to read. Identify the main argument put forward to explain how the Revolution gave power to the workers. Then, develop a counter-argument.

Interpretation offered by the extract:

_____

_____

Counter-argument:

_____

_____

_____

_____

EXTRACT B

From Sheila Fitzpatrick, The Russian Revolution, *page 144 (1994)*

Enormous numbers of workers were promoted directly into industrial management, became soviet or party officials, or were appointed as replacements for the 'class enemies' purged from central government. For members of this favoured group – 'sons of the working class', as they liked to call themselves in later years – the Revolution had indeed fulfilled its promises to give power to the proletariat and turn workers into masters of the state.

Social developments: religion, minorities, propaganda and cultural change

Religion

Marx had described religion as 'the opium of the people', used to keep the lower classes quiet. Lenin recognised that most Russians were very religious and he tolerated religious worship. However, he launched a campaign to weaken the power of the Orthodox Church: its lands were seized; Church schools were taken over (as were Muslim schools); monasteries were turned into schools, hospitals and prisons; many priests lost their lives. Under Stalin, the destruction of rural churches and the confiscation of bells, icons and relics aroused huge opposition and religious protesters were branded as 'kulaks'. By 1940, only 500 churches were open for worship, one per cent of the number in 1917.

Minorities

In 1917, the Bolsheviks promised national self-determination for the ethnic minorities. The Finns opted for independence but others were prevailed on not to do so. All the major national minorities were separately represented in the Communist Party. With the abolition of Tsarist anti-Semitic laws, the Jewish language of Yiddish became more widely used. However, Stalin made the Soviet Union into a more centralised state and, from 1938, Russian had to be taught in all schools and became the sole language of the Red Army.

Soviet culture

The October Revolution led to a burst of artistic creativity, particularly in literature and poetry, which Lenin encouraged. However, Lenin also believed that 'art and literature should serve the people'. Stalin was even clearer that culture should serve a social and political role, above all to promote socialist values. In the 1930s, this came to mean conforming to the standards set by Stalin (artists who did not conform were purged). He believed that writers were 'engineers of the human soul': art was not about free expression but about shaping Soviet society. The Soviet Union of Writers, to which all writers had to belong after 1934, insisted that all members should strive for 'socialist realism': they should ensure their work could be understood by the workers and contained characters who could be socialist role models or easily identified as class enemies. Above all, their message should be optimistic and uplifting.

Before his death in 1934, the writer Maxim Gorky praised Stalin's first Five-Year Plan as something of 'the highest spiritual value'. Other writers were not so accommodating and many were sent to labour camps or committed suicide. Many plays and films were withdrawn while the composer Shostakovich had to tread a very fine line after his opera, *Lady Macbeth of Mtsensk*, was banned.

Propaganda

Both Lenin and Stalin appreciated the value of propaganda, especially visual propaganda, for reaching the masses and winning them over to socialism. Stalin, in particular, exploited posters, cinema and radio: he was portrayed as the worthy successor to Lenin, as the hero and saviour of the Soviet people, a father figure guiding them through the years of collectivisation and industrialisation with the promise of a socialist paradise to come. This image of Stalin was manufactured by the Communist Party machine which controlled the media. Lenin had not sought to be an icon but Stalin definitely did: he became the personification of the nation and, in this way, he undoubtedly strengthened his power. (See page 80 on the 'personality cult' of Stalin.)

Complete the paragraph **a**

Below is a sample essay question and the outline of a paragraph written in answer to the question. The paragraph contains a point with some relevant comment and specific evidence but it lacks a concluding analytical link back to the question. Complete the paragraph by adding this link back to the question in the space provided.

'The Communist government succeeded in forcing all writers and artists to serve the Soviet state from 1917 to 1941.' Assess the validity of this view.

Under Lenin, writers and artists were allowed freedom of expression but Stalin set out to make them conform to the demands of 'socialist realism'. Their work had to be accessible to the workers and contribute to the development of a new, socialist society. However, some writers and artists refused to conform and their works, such as Shostakovich's opera *Lady MacBeth of Mtsensk*, were banned. This shows that ...

_____

_____

 Developing an argument

Below is a sample exam question, a list of key points to be made in the essay and a paragraph from the essay. Read the question, the plan and the sample paragraph. Rewrite the paragraph in order to develop an argument. Your paragraph should answer the question directly and set out the evidence that supports your argument. Crucially, it should develop an argument by setting out a general answer to the question and reasons that support this.

'A new Soviet society was created between 1917 and 1941.' Assess the validity of this view.

Key points:
- The suppression of religious practice
- Representation of national minorities but Russian made sole language of the army
- Artistic creativity directed towards 'socialist realism' under Stalin
- Propaganda portrayed Stalin as a saviour and the Soviet Union as a socialist paradise in the future.

Sample paragraph

Most Russians had been highly religious under the Tsars but churches and religious worship were suppressed in the Soviet Union. Instead, a heaven on earth was promised, with Stalin as a saviour and father figure who would oversee this transformation. Artistic endeavour was channelled into the production of socialist realist art and writing which portrayed happy workers and wicked bourgeois enemies.

Opposition: faction, terror and the purges

From their first days in power, the Bolsheviks faced opposition and thousands of 'anti-Bolsheviks' were sent to labour camps. During the Civil War, the Cheka implemented a Red Terror (see page 56) in order to destroy 'enemies of the people'. Then, in 1921, Lenin issued a 'ban on factions' in order to curb criticism of the government from within the party. Stalin exploited all of these methods but he intensified the element of terror in order to consolidate his own personal power. In eliminating actual or potential opponents, he also included fellow members of the Central Committee, which Lenin had never done.

Following the suicide of his wife in 1932 and growing criticism from within the party and government of the speed of collectivisation, Stalin increasingly feared that even his closest colleagues could betray him. Over the following year, almost a million members were excluded from the party and, from 1934, Stalin began a systematic purge of senior members of the party and government. The main purges were:

- 1934 **Kirov**, a popular figure and potential rival to Stalin, was killed. Stalin used this as the pretext for the arrest of members of what he called the Trotskyite and **Zinoviev–Kamenev** factions. Those purged were replaced with loyal Stalinists.
- 1936 Zinoviev and Kamenev, and 14 other Bolsheviks, were shot after a 'show trial' in which they confessed to treason and involvement in the murder of Kirov.
- 1937 Several Bolshevik leaders and most of the military and naval high command were shot.
- 1938 Bukharin, Rykov and more senior Bolsheviks, together with Yagoda, the former head of the **NKVD**, were shot.
- 1940 Trotsky was assassinated in Mexico.

From 1937 to 1938 onwards, the terror was increasingly directed at ordinary citizens. It became a method of government and the population were encouraged to inform on 'hidden enemies'. Quotas of victims to be arrested in every region were drawn up like industrial production targets and hundreds of thousands were executed or died in prison. Altogether, one in eighteen of the Soviet population was arrested during the purges.

One less well-known element of the purges was the campaign to deport national minorities, such as Poles and Germans, from the regions near the Soviet Union's western borders. This was carried out because of fears that these people might join an invading army. Over 100,000 Poles were shot during the campaign.

Stalin called a halt to the terror in November 1938 but the purges left most of the population frightened and bewildered. However, Stalin achieved his aim of eliminating all rivals, replacing them with ardent Stalinists, and of attaining absolute control over the party and the people.

A-level interpretation question

Below is an A-level-style question. Read the extracts and then plan an answer for each one of them.

Using your understanding of the historical context, assess how convincing the arguments in these three extracts are in relation to the use of terror from 1917 to 1941.

EXTRACT A

Adapted from Martin Sixsmith, Russia: A 1,000-Year Chronicle of the Wild East, *page 232 (2012)*

In response to the attack on Lenin [attempted assassination in 1918], so-called class enemies were rounded up and executed for no other crime than their social origin. Hostages were selected from former tsarist officials, landowners, priests, lawyers, bankers and merchants to be used as reprisals. Lenin himself signed the execution lists. The aim seemed to be the physical annihilation of a whole social class. Being modestly well off made you guilty; soft hands unused to manual labour could get you shot. The Bolsheviks relied more and more on the murderous henchmen of the Cheka. The organisation's methods were extrajudicial [not authorised by a court of law]: confessions extracted by torture followed by immediate execution. Cheka's leader, Felix Dzerzhinsky, claimed, 'this should be frankly admitted. Terror is an absolute necessity during times of revolution. Our aim is to fight against the enemies of the Soviet government and of the new order of life'.

EXTRACT B

Adapted from D. Volkogonov, The Rise and Fall of the Soviet Empire, *page 107 (1999)*

To understand why Stalin launched the great purge, it is important to understand that he was driven by a powerful need to win. He was obsessed by the idea of 'overtaking' everyone, of 'racing forward' a hundred years in ten. He told the Party in 1931: 'Either we do this or they [the capitalists] will crush us.' He was trying to outrun the natural course of events. People, however, change slowly. Soviet society, Stalin maintained, still harboured countless members of the old middle classes, former officers, unreconstructed members of the pre-1917 political parties, covert saboteurs and spies, and 'the sharpening of the class struggle' was at hand. The system needed a general purge, from which it would emerge stronger and more homogenous [of the same type], and hence able to speed up 'the transition to the second phase of Communism'. For the Stalinist system to function on all levels, for it to achieve its economic, social and political goals, permanent purge was a necessity. The entire period of Stalin's rule was a bloody one, though the 1930s saw the worst excesses, as Stalin sought to secure a greater 'moral and political unity of society'. The population, silent except when told to shout the slogan of the day, was made to expose and 'uproot' a seemingly endless succession of hostile groups.

EXTRACT C

Adapted from O. Figes, Revolutionary Russia, 1891–1991, *page 191 (2014)*

The Great Terror was a complex amalgam of different elements: the purging of the Party, the great 'show trials', the mass arrests in the cities, the 'kulak operation' and 'national operations' against minorities. But while it may be helpful to analyse these various components separately, the fact remains that they all began and ended simultaneously, which does suggest that they were part of a unified campaign that needs to be explained. To begin to understand, we must look at the Great Terror as an operation masterminded and controlled by Stalin directly in response to the circumstances he perceived in 1937.

There were many waves of terror in the Stalin period – the arrests of 'bourgeois specialists', 'wreckers', and 'saboteurs' during the industrial terror, the mass repressions of the 'kulaks' and their families, the trials of 'Zinovievites' and 'Trotskyists' in Stalin's battles with the Bolsheviks but it was not just a routine wave of mass arrests, isolating 'enemies' by sending them to camps, but a calculated policy of mass killing. Stalin wanted to eliminate any 'anti-Soviet elements' that could become a 'fifth column' [people sympathetic to an enemy, who might join an invading army]. By 1937, Stalin was convinced that war was imminent and concluded that political repression was required in the Soviet Union to crush all potential opposition before the outbreak of a war with the fascists.

3 The emergence of communist dictatorship, 1917–41

The Soviet Union by 1941

Stalin's rule

- Stalin had encouraged great reverence for Lenin and portrayed himself as continuing the work of his predecessor. He identified loyalty to Lenin with loyalty to the party. Furthermore, by the late 1920s, he had succeeded in identifying his own authority with that of the party. This made opposition to Stalin appear like opposition to Lenin, the party and the Revolution.

- Many of the key features of Stalinist rule had been established by Lenin: one-party rule, the secret police, the use of terror and show trials. Lenin had said that the task of the Bolsheviks was 'the ruthless destruction of the enemy'. Stalin continued Lenin's 'class warfare', particularly directed against the kulaks and the bourgeoisie. In many ways, Stalin's rule was simply a more fully developed and repressive form of Lenin's highly authoritarian rule.

- However, the purges constituted a complete break with the Bolshevik Revolution and Lenin's regime and they led to the development of a highly personal form of rule. Stalin replaced the old Bolsheviks whom he eliminated with a new class of officials, the **nomenklatura**, who were completely loyal to him. They had no loyalty to the Bolshevik Revolution and its leaders. They were completely Stalin's men. Their positions depended on him as did the rights and privileges – the luxurious apartments, the plentiful food, the cars – that came with them. They were unlikely to doubt or criticise their leader. The party congress which met in 1939 was completely subservient to Stalin.

- Nevertheless, there were limits to Stalin's power, not least in the thousands of officials on whom he depended to implement his policies. The impact of his policies in the regions could be moderated by local conditions, the effects of corruption and, in the case of the purges, by the desire to settle old scores and fill the shoes of those eliminated.

The economy

The Soviet Union had undergone an economic transformation by 1941. It was fast becoming an industrialised, urban society. The development of heavy industry and large building projects enabled the country to withstand the onslaught of Nazi Germany. However, the production of consumer goods was neglected; agriculture failed to recover from the crisis of collectivisation and was still not producing as much grain in 1941 as it had done under the NEP.

Social life

By 1941, nearly all peasants lived and worked in the **kolkhoz**, supervised by party officials. Millions of peasants had moved to the cities, become educated and benefited from state welfare services. However, food was scarce and housing overcrowded. With priority given to rearmament from the late 1930s, living and working conditions became harsher. Yet the burden was not shared equally. Far from being classless, Stalinist society had become hierarchical, with a privileged elite of party and government officials, military and police officers, and some workers (e.g. Stakhanovites) rewarded with higher pay and other benefits.

! RAG – rate the timeline

Below is a sample exam question and a timeline. Read the question, study the timeline and, using three coloured pens, put a red, amber or green star next to the events to show:
- Red: Events and policies that have no relevance to the question
- Amber: Events and policies that have some significance to the question
- Green: Events and policies that are directly relevant to the question

'The Soviet Union underwent far greater transformation under Stalin than it did under Lenin in the years from 1917 to 1941.' To what extent do you agree with this assessment?

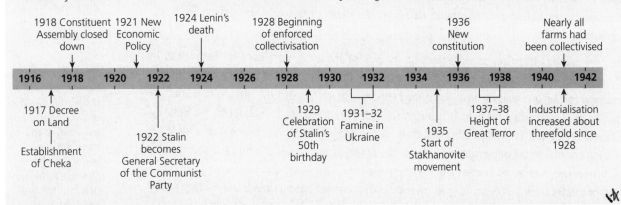

How far do you agree? a

Read the following extract on the Soviet achievement by 1941. Summarise the main arguments and then add your own knowledge to agree with or contradict each of the arguments.

EXTRACT A

Adapted from John Gooding, Rulers and Subjects: Government and People in Russia, 1801–1991, *page 210 (1996)*

By 1940, industrial production was about three times what it had been at the start of the first Five-Year Plan. That showed what could be done when ruthless government went together with an explosion of working-class energy in pursuit of an earthly heaven. The peasantry had been conquered; nature too had been tamed in the service of socialism; and the rise of great industrial complexes amidst the forest and steppe triumphantly proclaimed that there were indeed no fortresses which party and working class together could not take ... What happened at the top was mirrored in the rise of a legion of little Stalins who drove the revolution forward in the localities. The little Stalins in turn depended on the zeal and energy of party militants, and since they needed ever more of them, still more workers were recruited to the party. By 1932, 65 per cent of a total membership of more than three million were workers by origin and as many as 44 per cent were workers by actual occupation. The party had never been before, and would never be again, such a bastion of the working class. The worker-militants' agenda was very largely at this stage what the leadership wanted: to build socialism, make the revolution irreversible, and destroy whatever remained of the old order.

Exam focus (A-level)

Below is a sample A-level essay written to a good Level 4 standard. It was written in response to an A-level question. Read it and the comments around it.

'The peasantry suffered greatly throughout the period 1914–41.' Assess the validity of this view.

For most of the period 1914–41, the majority of the peasantry suffered greatly. There was some relief in 1917–18 and then again during the NEP, before the peasantry were to experience the period of most intense suffering, the years of collectivisation from 1928 onwards.

In 1914, millions of peasants, who made up the bulk of the army, were sent to the front in the First World War. Poorly fed, led, clothed and armed, they were treated as little better than cannon fodder and millions died. After the February Revolution of 1917, there was a brief period of respite when the peasants began to seize the nobles' land. In October, the Bolshevik Decree on Land effectively legitimised what was already taking place: the peasants were taking control of the countryside. However the onset of the Civil War led to the policy of War Communism: in order to extract more grain to feed the Red Army and the factory workers, the peasants were subjected to grain requisitioning, carried out by Cheka and military units which seized grain and shot 'hoarders'. The kulaks, many of whom had made considerable profits from farming, were portrayed as 'enemies of the people', and were particularly hard-hit, often having all their stock seized. However, it would be true to say that the vast majority of peasants, not just the kulaks, suffered during the Civil War and many retreated into subsistence farming, which in turn contributed to widespread famine in 1921.

The period of the NEP brought some relief from the exploitation of the war years. There were to be no more forced seizures by grain requisitioning squads. Furthermore, the peasants were encouraged to grow more food with the incentive of being allowed to sell their surplus for profit. Many peasants benefited, the kulak class in particular. However, the Communist government regularly increased the size of the grain quotas which the peasants were required to hand over as tax. Meanwhile, a lack of consumer goods in the shops meant the peasants had little incentive to grow more grain as there was little to buy and many reverted to subsistence farming. This situation, and a desire to transform the Soviet Union into a modern, industrialised nation, led to Stalin's decision to collectivise Soviet agriculture. In order to achieve Socialism in One Country, he set out to win the 'battle for grain' and extract enough grain to pay for the industrialisation of the Soviet Union. Thus began the period of harshest and most blatant exploitation of the peasantry.

In Stalin's drive for collectivisation, from 1928 onwards, the peasants were herded, by officials backed up by troops, into kolkhozy. They were forced to hand over their crops and their livestock to the collectives, which were run by officials who often had little knowledge of farming. Millions resisted, burning their crops and killing their livestock rather than hand them over. They were branded as kulaks. Most of those identified as kulaks were the more hard-working, efficient farmers but the notion of a kulak class also provided grounds for the coercion of the peasantry as a whole. The land and property of the better-off farmers were seized and millions were driven into forced labour camps to build the new, industrialised Soviet paradise. Families were broken up and children left uncared for. Even while peasants starved in Ukraine in 1932–33, grain was exported to pay for the import of Western technology and to feed the fast-growing industrial workforce. Furthermore, the famine was kept a secret from the urban workforce and foreign journalists. Machine tractor stations were established,

A short, clear introduction which indicates the line of argument to be developed.

Brief, pertinent reference to the suffering of the war years with which to contrast the relief which the 1917 Revolution brought for the peasantry. Then, with appropriate evidence in support, this paragraph identifies the short period of intense exploitation, particularly of the kulaks.

The counter-argument to the assertion in the title is developed and well supported. Then, this line of argument is qualified. Finally, the marked change of direction in Soviet policy is pinpointed, leading to support for the contention contained in the title.

ostensibly to provide seed and tractors to make agriculture more productive, as well as to control the countryside, but not enough tractors were made and the collective farms were badly organised. Ten-year prison sentences were introduced for stealing from a collective or for attempting to sell grain before quotas were filled. By 1939, the vast majority of farms had been collectivised and the traditional peasant's way of life, based on the family farm, the commune and the Church, had been destroyed. The government did make one concession to the peasants: it allowed them to keep small, private plots of land where they could grow food to sell in the market. Nevertheless, many peasants would refer to the period of collectivisation, from 1928 to 1941, as 'second serfdom'.

The largely urban-educated Communist leadership (even Stalin, who came from peasant stock) had little knowledge or understanding of the peasantry. They were mostly contemptuous of the peasants, despising them for what they saw as their petty-capitalist mentality. The factory workers were the heroes of the Revolution, the builders of the new, socialist society, not the peasantry. Despite a brief period in 1917–18 and during the NEP years from 1921 to 1928, the peasants suffered greatly in the years from 1914 to 1941, never more so than during the Stalin years of collectivisation.

> A well-developed explanation to support the argument identified in the introduction. Plentiful, accurate, relevant evidence is competently deployed to substantiate the argument.

> A sound final paragraph, with pertinent contextual explanation and a clear conclusion.

Shows good understanding of the question and is well organised and clearly explained. There is much specific, accurate, well-selected evidence in support of the arguments, showing a high level of understanding. However, although it is explanatory throughout, it is rather too narrative in structure, hence high Level 4 rather than Level 5.

Find the evidence

The most important element in producing an argument is supporting evidence and examples. Read the essay again and identify where evidence has been used effectively to support a point.

4 The Stalinist dictatorship and reaction, 1941–64

The Soviet Union in wartime: Stalin, political authority and opposition

The impact of the invasion

On 22 June 1941, Nazi Germany invaded the Soviet Union in what was the largest German military operation of the Second World War. Stalin was taken by surprise and his government was unprepared for war with so many senior officers purged in the 1930s.

- Within 24 hours, 1,200 Soviet aircraft were destroyed on the ground.
- After three weeks, a million troops were killed or injured and 20 million were living under German rule.
- There was a danger that the regime might collapse in the midst of defeat, as the Tsarist regime had done.

Yet, once roused and mobilised, the sheer ruthlessness of a highly centralised regime was turned to advantage and a highly effective wartime government emerged. The war was conducted by a small group, the State Defence Committee. Stalin put himself in overall military command but he had the good sense, unlike Hitler, to leave his generals free to direct the military campaigns. Stalin's first wartime speech addressed his 'brothers and sisters', not the more usual Soviet 'comrades', and he appealed, in the name of the 'motherland', to their sense of Russian nationalism, not their loyalty to the Soviet Union or to communism. This was to be the 'Great Patriotic War'.

Wartime opposition

Hitler had hoped that large numbers of non-Russian national minorities (e.g. in Ukraine and the Baltic republics) would rise up against Stalin. There was no widespread uprising but thousands who had suffered in the 1930s did collaborate with the German forces. Stalin's response was to transfer over a million people, from different ethnic groups, simply because he suspected they were or might be disloyal. Ukrainians, Germans and Chechens were among those who were uprooted and moved east. Thus, the purges continued in wartime. Terror was also exploited on the front line: when Stalingrad was on the verge of defeat in 1942, Stalin ordered that deserters and 'cowards', any who tried to retreat, were to be shot. Within a few weeks, 13,000 were executed for such 'crimes'.

Others who came under suspicion were returning prisoners of war in 1945. They were seen as potentially disloyal because they had become tainted by Western values while in captivity. Many were transferred directly to the Soviet labour camps.

The political impact of the war

Stalin addressed the grievances of the army officers by reducing the role of the political commissars attached to army units, and he restored special badges of rank. Also, vast numbers among the armed forces were encouraged to join the Communist Party so that, by the end of the war, half the members were from the army and navy. Although nationalism was emphasised in wartime propaganda, Stalin declared that the victory over Germany was a victory for communism over fascism. The idea of the 'people's war' was played down and the 'Great Patriotic War' was hailed as a victory for Stalin and the Soviet socialist system.

How far do you agree?

Read the following extract on Stalin's conduct of the war. Summarise the main arguments and then add your own knowledge to agree with or contradict each of the arguments.

EXTRACT A

Adapted from D. Volkogonov, The Rise and Fall of the Soviet Empire, *page 114 (1999)*

There was little possibility of sober collective judgement while Stalin was the subject of such total adulation. He believed that his judgement and wishes coincided with the real needs of the Party and country which he ruled like an absolute monarch. The appalling suffering inflicted on the Soviet people in the war was no less the result of German force and treachery than of major mistakes by the Soviet leadership. Stalin exacerbated the already extreme violence of war by pursuing his customary methods of ruling. He was extricated from his disastrous miscalculation, not only by the unprecedented self-sacrifice of the Soviet people, but also by the mass Terror applied to those who wavered or lost support. The effect of Stalin's savagery in the early months of the war was to make the people dig their heels in, summon up all their courage, and overcome their faint-heartedness through fear of the mortal punishment they knew he would mete out.

Developing an argument

Below is a sample exam question, a list of key points to be made in the essay and a paragraph from the essay. Read the question, the plan and the sample paragraph. Rewrite the paragraph in order to develop an argument. Your paragraph should answer the question directly and set out the evidence that supports your argument. Crucially, it should develop an argument by setting out a general answer to the question and reasons that support this.

'The nature of Stalin's rule changed little during the Second World War.' Assess the validity of this view in the context of the period from 1928 to 1945.

Key points:

- Appealed more to love of country than need to defend communism
- Increasingly allowed generals to conduct military campaigns
- Continued use of terror, especially in the army and with ethnic minorities
- Continued to give priority to heavy industry and production of weapons.

Sample paragraph

Stalin continued to make use of terror as a method of government during the war. It was used, for instance, on the frontline at Stalingrad in order to deter soldiers from retreating. Also, it was used to transfer many Ukrainians and Germans living in the Soviet Union, some of whom allied with the invaders. In this way, Stalin carried on using terror as he had done in the 1930s.

AQA AS/A-level History Tsarist and Communist Russia 1855–1964   75

4 The Stalinist dictatorship and reaction, 1941–64

The Soviet Union in wartime: the economic and social impact

Economic impact

By the end of August 1941, Leningrad (previously St Petersburg, then Petrograd) was surrounded and besieged. By October, German forces were on the outskirts of Moscow. Fifty per cent of the country's coal, iron and steel was in German hands. The fate of the Soviet Union hung in the balance. It required a massive military effort but also the mobilisation of all the available economic resources in order to halt the Nazi onslaught. Fortunately for the survival of the Soviet people, the economy had effectively been put on a war footing in the Five-Year Plans. The emphasis on heavy industry and armaments, and the highly centralised nature of the system, were of great value in organising the war effort. One of the greatest achievements was the huge evacuation of people to, and the rapid creation of military-industrial plants in, the Ural mountains and further east, beyond the reach of the German forces. This was where the planned economy was triumphant, where 'the revolution won the war', in the words of historian Orlando Figes. Without state coercion this could not have been achieved in so little time.

- Thousands of factories were moved east or built anew.
- Nearly all industrial production was geared towards military needs.
- Railways were built to connect new industrial bases with the war fronts.
- Factories were put under martial law to tighten labour discipline and productivity.
- Harsh punishments were given for poor work or lateness.
- A 72-hour week became the norm.
- Strict rationing was introduced.
- By 1943 industrial production exceeded Germany's.
- The USA provided thousands of planes, tanks and military vehicles and 5 million tons of food.

Prison camp labour produced much weaponry as well as most of the army's uniforms. Prisoners could be and were worked to death. A similar disregard was shown for individual human lives in the army: strategic goals were set no matter how many lives would be lost to achieve them. This may explain why 8.6 million troops lost their lives in the war.

Social impact

- Over 25 million lives were lost, mostly civilian, many through starvation.
- Leningrad was besieged for over two years, with no heating, no lighting and no water supply.
- Eight hundred thousand died in the city in the winter of 1941–42, more than combined US/UK losses during the whole war.
- Propaganda emphasised patriotism to drive the invader out of Mother Russia.
- Most people responded, ready to undergo extreme hardship rather than surrender.
- Most had experienced and survived harsh conditions in the 1930s and were prepared to do so again for the sake of a brighter future.
- With the countryside stripped of men, horses and machinery, four out of five collective farmers were women, often pulling ploughs by hand.
- The churches were allowed to reopen and did much to raise morale and support the war to defend 'Holy Mother Russia'.
- Government propaganda exploited nationalist feeling, invoking memories of great Russian heroes of the Tsarist past as well as of the Civil War.
- The war brought government and people together and Stalin emerged as the nation's saviour, held in even greater awe and fear than before.

ⓘ Use own knowledge to support or contradict ⓐ

Below is an extract to read. Identify the main argument put forward to explain Soviet victory in the war. Then, develop a counter-argument.

EXTRACT A

Adapted from J. P. Nettl, The Soviet Achievement *(1967)*

When the war was all over, Stalin thanked 'the Russian people for their confidence in their government'. This was only a minimal recognition of the truth. The Germans had helped to make his task much easier. They showed unparalleled brutality to the population of the occupied territories, to the many prisoners they had captured. Their determination to exploit the Soviet Union as a source of food and slave labour for the German war effort undermined the effectiveness of anti-communist propaganda.

ⓘ Turning assertion into argument ⓐ

Below is a sample A-level essay question and a series of assertions. Read the question and then add a justification to each of the assertions to turn it into a supported view, so creating an argument.

To what extent did the Second World War change the nature of the Soviet economy and society? Answer with reference to the period 1928 to 1945.

The priority given to heavy industry after 1928 was maintained during the war

_____

_____

There was a massive transfer and rebuilding of industrial plants in the Ural mountains

_____

_____

Working conditions in industry became harsher

_____

_____

Most workers on the collective farms were women

_____

_____

The churches played a significant part in rallying support for the war effort

_____

_____

High Stalinism and the revival of terror

Most of the Soviet people had made huge sacrifices during the war in the hope of securing a better future. Yet their hopes were to be dashed. After the end of the war, there was a new enemy, the USA, and Russians had to prepare for a new international struggle, the **Cold War**. There would be no reform after 1945. Instead, the country had to be sealed off from the West. Censorship was increased and the NKVD was strengthened.

Although Stalin's rule appeared to be stronger as a result of victory in war, he still feared rivals. In order to strengthen his control yet further, he abolished the State Defence Committee. In particular, he demoted several high-ranking army generals as a way of putting the military in their place. Marshal Zhukov, hugely popular and therefore, in Stalin's eyes, a rival, was posted far away from Moscow. Stalin made himself Defence Minister. As he grew older, he became even more suspicious of those around him. He dispensed with the Central Committee and the Politburo, thus removing any semblance of limitation upon his authority. There was not another party congress until 1952. Stalin relied increasingly on his private advisers in order to bypass both party and government bodies and to exert his own absolute authority.

Terror and the destruction of 'supposed opposition'

Stalin revived the use of terror as a political weapon. The terror did not reach pre-war levels but many thousands were executed every year for 'counter-revolutionary' activities. Two of the more significant purges were:

- The 'Leningrad Affair': In 1949, Stalin turned on the Leningrad party organisation. Its leaders showed a strong sense of independence and solidarity, developed during the wartime siege. Two of the leaders were seen as possible successors to Stalin (he was now 70). This was enough for Stalin to have several arrested, forced to confess and shot.
- The 'Doctors' Plot': The Cold War bred an intense fear of foreigners. A Soviet citizen could be arrested for even brief contact with a foreigner. Stalin was particularly suspicious of the 2 million Soviet Jews. He had supported the new Jewish state of Israel, created in 1948, hoping it would become a Soviet ally but, when it turned out to be pro-American, he became afraid of pro-Israeli feeling among Soviet Jews, seeing them as a potential threat. In 1952, Stalin announced a conspiracy by the Kremlin doctors to murder him and other Soviet leaders. Seven of the nine 'white-coated assassins' were Jewish. Hundreds of doctors were arrested and tortured into making confessions. Then thousands of ordinary Jews were arrested and deported to remote parts of the country where new labour camps were built to contain them. Anti-Jewish feeling was whipped up in the press. Then, at the height of the hysteria, Stalin died on 5 March 1953.

(i) Develop the detail a

Below is a sample exam question, followed by a series of statements to be used in an answer. Add relevant, specific detail to each of the statements in order to increase the value of the answer.

'Throughout the years 1928–53, Stalin used fear of the West as the main justification for the autocratic nature of his rule.' To what extent do you agree with this view?

- Fear of the West was part of the justification for the purges of the mid-1930s and the transfer of millions of ethnic minority people before and during the war years.
- It was partly fear of the West and the need to catch up that led Stalin to establish the Five-Year Plans.
- However, fear of the West was not the primary reason for massive, swift collectivisation from the late 1920s. It was carried out, on Stalin's orders, in order to show that communism worked.
- Above all, however, Stalin ruled autocratically because he feared rivals, especially from 1934 onwards.

(i) Introducing and concluding an argument a

Read the A-level exam essay title below.

Look at the key points of the answer.

How good is the proposed introduction?

How effective is the proposed conclusion?

Could either be improved, especially to reach Level 5? (See page 7 for mark scheme.)

To what extent was terror used as a political weapon in the years from 1928 to 1953?

Key points:

- Terror was exploited less in the late 1920s and early 1930s.
- It was used most extensively from 1934 to 1938 and the purges were called off in 1938.
- Terror was used in wartime on the front line and in the mass movement of minorities.
- Its use on the civilian population was revived after 1945.

Introduction

Terror was used most extensively during the purges of the mid-1930s, reaching its height in 1937–38, but it was used throughout the period. Terror was exploited in the late 1920s and early 1930s, as it had been in Lenin's years, but not on anything like the scale of the mid- to late 1930s. In wartime, many soldiers were executed for cowardice and millions of national minorities were moved east, with huge numbers dying on the way. Then, the use of terror was revived in the late 1940s.

Conclusion

In conclusion, terror was used for political purposes throughout the period. Its use reached its height in the Great Terror of 1937–38 but it was also used to a lesser extent in Stalin's early years and in the Second World War.

High Stalinism and the 'cult of personality'

Both before and even more so during the war, Stalin was portrayed not just as the leader but as the very embodiment of the nation. He was increasingly recognised, especially after victory in 1945, as 'the father of the peoples of the USSR'. Furthermore, Stalin the Georgian was portrayed as a great Russian, following in a line of heroes from Ivan the Terrible, Peter the Great and, of course, Lenin. Stalin's birthday became the biggest celebration in the Soviet calendar, with flags bearing his image, like a religious icon, carried in procession in Red Square in Moscow.

This 'cult of personality' reached its height after the war. Stalin was portrayed not only as a man of exceptional genius but also as a 'man of the people', ever-present, all-knowing and benevolent towards his people. On his 70th birthday, a giant portrait of Stalin was suspended in the sky over Moscow and lit up at night by search lights.

The power vacuum on Stalin's death

When Stalin's death was announced in March 1953, prisoners in the labour camps may have rejoiced at the news but, across the country, there was widespread and genuine grief. There was also alarm at the prospect of a future without Stalin: he had been Russia's saviour in the war and, in the years since, had represented stability in an uncertain world. The poet Yevtushenko later wrote, 'All Russia wept. So did I'. Andrei Sakharov, who would later be an outspoken critic of the Soviet regime, was overcome by 'the great man's death'. Only later would he realise the true nature of the Stalinist system and the extent to which he had been deceived. Meanwhile, Stalin was laid to rest next to Lenin.

Stalin had been increasingly frail in his later years but had made no attempt to prepare a successor. Far from it, he continued to play off his ministers against one another, encouraging rivalry between contenders for the leadership, so great was his fear of threats to his personal rule. When he finally called a party congress in 1952, speeches were made by Politburo members **Georgy Malenkov** and **Nikita Khrushchev** and it was announced that the Politburo would be replaced by a larger Presidium. Some suspected that Stalin was preparing for another purge by raising up new members to senior positions. When Stalin did die, there was no clear successor. However, the three main contenders for power appeared to be **Lavrenty Beria**, head of the secret police, Malenkov and **Vyacheslav Molotov**.

How far do you agree?

Read the following extract on the challenge facing Stalin's successors. Summarise the main arguments and then add your own knowledge to agree with or contradict each of the arguments.

EXTRACT A

Adapted from Robert Service, A History of Modern Russia, *page 330 (1997)*

There were several problems left behind by Stalin: in politics, economy, ethnic relations, culture, security, and continental and global power. And they complicated and aggravated each other. It is true that the Soviet order was not on the verge of collapse but if several of these problems were not tackled within the next few years, a fundamental crisis would occur. Stalin's associates were justified in feeling nervous, and knew that the next few months would be a period of great trial for them. The uncontainable surge of the crowds on to the streets of Red Square in Moscow as Stalin was laid to rest had been a warning to Stalin's successors about the passions lurking under society's calm surface. This was the first act of self-assertion by the people since the inception of Stalin's dictatorship. It was by no means clear how the Kremlin leaders would respond to the challenge. They wanted to consolidate their positions of power as individuals and to preserve the Soviet order. Their common goals were to maintain the one-party, one-ideology state, to expand its economy, to control all public institutions and their personnel, and to mobilise the rest of society. And several of these veterans were convinced that these goals were unattainable unless a reform programme was quickly to be implemented.

Developing an argument

Below is a sample exam question, a list of key points to be made in the essay and a paragraph from the essay. Read the question, the plan and the sample paragraph. Rewrite the paragraph in order to develop an argument. Your paragraph should answer the question directly and set out the evidence that supports your argument. Crucially, it should develop an argument by setting out a general answer to the question and reasons that support this.

'The nature of Stalin's rule changed little in the period 1928 to 1953.' Assess the validity of this view.

Key points:
- The Soviet Union was a one-party state, heavily reliant on the secret police, throughout.
- Stalin established his own personal dominance early on, increasing it steadily after 1934.
- The 'cult of personality' was developed in the 1930s and intensified after the war.
- Stalin made use of terror, particularly from 1934 to 1938, to the end of his life.

Sample paragraph

Stalin was personally dominant, equating his rule with that of the party, throughout. He inherited a one-party state with a secret police and made increasing use of the latter in the 1930s. The cult of personality was developed in the 1930s, making particularly effective use of visual propaganda. Terror was used as a political weapon, to eliminate Bolshevik leaders and then ordinary people, especially from 1934 onwards, and its use was revived after the war.

Political authority and government: Khrushchev, 1953–64

Khrushchev's rise to power

Stalin's death was followed by a period of collective leadership, yet differences over policy and personal rivalries were a sign of a power struggle behind the scenes. Beria was the dominant figure and immediately presented himself as a reformer. He issued an amnesty leading to the release of a million prisoners, mostly criminals rather than political prisoners. However, senior party officials as well as military leaders feared him and were suspicious of his intentions. They conspired to arrange for his arrest, which was carried out by the military. Beria was blamed for the worst excesses of Stalinist rule, tried and shot. The coup which led to his downfall was organised by Nikita Khrushchev, General Secretary of the party. Khrushchev emerged with new authority although, as a man from a peasant background with little schooling, he was not initially seen as a threat by other leaders. However, like Stalin, he used his position as General Secretary to build up a power base in the party.

Malenkov, the Prime Minister, proposed popular economic measures to boost the production of consumer goods and reform agriculture. However, he was blamed for a poor harvest in 1953. Khrushchev, seeing himself as the expert on agriculture, proposed his Virgin Lands scheme (see page 84), which met with early success. He also allied himself with heavy industry and army leaders, who disliked Malenkov's policies, and forced Malenkov to resign as head of the government in 1955.

De-Stalinisation

In February 1956, Khrushchev gave a 'secret speech' to a closed session of the 20th Congress of the Communist Party. The speech was made to:
- break the hold which Stalin held over Soviet Russia
- allow the new leadership to move on and make changes
- absolve Khrushchev and other leaders of complicity in Stalin's terror.

Khrushchev criticised Stalin for his 'abuses of power', blamed him personally for the terror and, above all, attacked the 'cult of personality', implying that all the deaths of innocent people were a result of Stalin's 'mania for greatness'. However, Khrushchev's list of innocent victims did not go back before 1934 because the aim of the speech was to blacken Stalin's reputation, not to blame the Communist Party from which Khrushchev and other leaders derived their authority. The aim was to restore faith in the party, the party of Lenin.

Some observers saw 'de-Stalinisation' as the start of a new era of tolerance and freedom. Over 2 million prisoners, including many 'politicals', were released from the camps by 1960 (although millions more never returned home) and there was some easing of censorship (see page 86) but the Soviet Union remained a one-party state with a secret police (now called the KGB), even if the latter's power was now diminished. Some of those party members who later heard about the speech asked why the leaders had not spoken out earlier about Stalin's terror. The more radical critics were expelled from the party as 'rotten elements'.

Spectrum of importance

Below is a sample exam question and a series of statements relevant to the question. Use your own knowledge and the information on the previous pages to reach a judgement about the importance of these points to the question posed.

Write numbers on the spectrum below to indicate the relative importance of the statements. Having done this, write a brief justification of your placement, explaining why some of these factors are more important than others. The resulting diagram could form the basis of an essay plan.

'Khrushchev's "secret speech" was a major turning point in the Soviet politics of the period from 1941 to 1964.' Explain whether you agree or disagree with this view.

1 No Soviet leader had dared to speak out about the purges until the speech.

2 The speech was criticised by some hardliners in the Soviet leadership.

3 The speech broke the hold which Stalin had exercised for 25 years.

4 The speech was accompanied by a thaw that led to the release of millions of prisoners.

5 Terror was never to be used systematically again by Soviet rulers.

6 The speech led to the policy of 'peaceful co-existence' with the West.

7 The speech led to a permanent easing of censorship.

8 The Soviet Union remained a one-party state with a network of spies and informers.

←──→

Least important   Most important

Turning assertion into argument

Below is a sample A-level essay question and a series of assertions. Read the question and then add a justification to each of the assertions to turn it into a supported view, so creating an argument.

How far did the nature of Soviet government change in the years from 1941 to 1964?

Government was highly centralised during the war and terror was a key component.

_____

_____

Stalin's rule became more of a personal dictatorship in his final years from 1945 to 1953.

_____

_____

In the Khrushchev years there was significant change, especially following the 'secret speech'.

_____

_____

Despite the 'thaw', the Soviet Union remained a highly authoritarian, one-party state.

_____

Economic developments, 1945–64

The economy under Stalin

After the hardship and suffering experienced in wartime, most Russians hoped for better after 1945. Instead, there was a return to the Five-Year Plans. In order to rebuild the devastated economy and rearm the country for the new Cold War era, priority was again given to heavy industry and defence, not consumer goods, and to the rebuilding of Soviet infrastructure. The war had destroyed 1,710 towns, 70,000 villages and 30,000 factories, and 100,000 collective farms had stopped working. After 1945, factories and steel works were rebuilt and mines reopened. Within a few years, the production of coal and steel passed 1940 levels. In 1949, an atomic bomb was tested, a significant technological achievement showing that the Soviet Union was catching up on the USA.

This was achieved by the imposition of longer hours and harsher discipline in the factories. Also, the prison camps, the population of which rose by a million from 1945 to 1950, provided an army of unpaid labour. In the countryside, the peasants continued to be squeezed. The state took up to 70 per cent of the peasants' grain, leaving barely enough for them to feed themselves, and paid low prices for it. Meanwhile, grain exports were increased to pay for spending on industry and the military. There was famine again in the countryside: over a million died in 1946–47.

The economy under Khrushchev

Khrushchev recognised the need to raise the standard of living of Soviet citizens, to tackle the poverty of the peasantry and the housing shortage. In other words, he wanted to bring about the material advancement promised by early Soviet leaders. He increased the payment made to peasants for their grain and cut the taxes they had to pay. He also launched a big house-building programme.

The Virgin Lands scheme

One of his primary aims was to solve the chronic food shortages by developing vast areas of previously uncultivated, 'virgin and idle' land in Siberia and Kazakhstan. About 300,000, mostly young, party enthusiasts were mobilised to go east and become pioneers of Khrushchev's plan. At first, the scheme was a great success and overall Soviet grain production rose by 75 per cent in four years from 1954 to 1958. However:
- Much of the new land was on the edge of desert and subject to drought.
- The soil was not properly prepared or fertilised.
- The top soil became arid, subject to wind erosion.
- The scheme was poorly planned and implemented too hastily.
- The management was ineffective and inefficient.
- There was poor housing for the volunteers and, as enthusiasm waned, many drifted back to the more comfortable life of the cities.

In 1963, the Soviet Union had to import large amounts of grain from North America in order to avoid famine.

Industry

Khrushchev recognised the need for a modern, technologically developed industry if the Soviet Union was going to 'catch up with and overtake America' and to show that communism worked. Investment in oil and natural gas was increased, as was the production of consumer goods. By the late 1950s, the economy was growing much faster than that of the USA. In 1957, the Soviets launched the first satellite into orbit and Soviet prestige was further enhanced when, in 1961, Yuri Gagarin became the first man in space.

Khrushchev reorganised the management of the economy in order to give more control to the actual producers: 11,000 factories were transferred from central government to regional government control. This devolution also strengthened the power of the party, at the expense of the economic ministries in Moscow, and increased Khrushchev's power and control. However, the increasing costs of defence and space exploration led to slower growth in the early 1960s.

Use own knowledge to support or contradict   a

Below is an extract to read. Identify the main argument put forward to explain agricultural development under Khrushchev. Then, develop a counter-argument.

EXTRACT A

Adapted from Edward Acton, Russia – The Tsarist and Soviet Legacy, *page 275 (1995)*

The growth in agricultural production left the stagnation of Stalinist days far behind. Under Khrushchev, the main source of increased output was the 'virgin lands' campaign of 1954-56. It gave a major short-term boost to output. In addition, from being a major source of funds for industry, agriculture became a major recipient. Procurement prices paid by the State for grain were sharply raised in an attempt to improve incentives and there was a large increase in the wages of workers on state farms.

i **Introducing and concluding an argument**   a

Read the A-level exam essay title below. Look at the key points of the answer. How good is the proposed introduction? How effective is the proposed conclusion? Could either be improved, especially to reach Level 5? (See page 7 for mark scheme.)

To what extent do you agree that industry was developed and agriculture was neglected throughout the years from 1941 to 1964?

Key points:

- Massive transfer, and development, of industrial plants during the war
- Emphasis on heavy industry and defence after the war as factories were rebuilt
- Agriculture squeezed both during and after the war and more dependent on female labour

- More investment in and production of consumer goods, oil and gas in Khrushchev years
- High priority given to agriculture, as in the Virgin Lands scheme
- Major developments in space technology.

Introduction

Heavy industry was given priority over consumer goods and agriculture until the Khrushchev years. This was in order to win the war against Germany and the Cold War. Significant achievements were made in space technology after the war. Agriculture became increasingly dependent on female labour throughout the Stalin years and the peasants were forced to hand over more grain, and were often paid less for it, even in the peacetime years. However, under Khrushchev, consumer goods and agriculture both increased production.

Conclusion

In conclusion, agriculture was squeezed in order to serve the interests of heavy industry and defence throughout the period although the Virgin Lands scheme was made a priority during the Khrushchev years.

Social and cultural developments, 1945–64

Social life under Stalin, 1945–53	Cultural life under Stalin, 1945–53
• Very little improvement in living standards • Few consumer goods and housing remained poor and in short supply • 12-hour working day remained the norm • The pay of a kolkhoz worker was one-sixth of that of a factory worker.	• Stalin was determined that the Soviet culture should be seen as superior to that of the liberal West • This anti-Westernism shaped policy towards the arts • Writers and artists were attacked for showing signs of 'bourgeois', non-Soviet, values.

Social change under Khrushchev, 1953–64

Khrushchev was a 'true believer' in communism, determined to show that it could achieve a better life for ordinary people.

- He gave higher priority to consumer goods and housing, especially to show that the Soviet Union compared well with the West.
- Fridges and TV sets began to appear in Soviet homes.
- Wage differences were reduced so that there was not such a gulf between the pay of managers and workers.
- The minimum wage was increased.
- Pensions were expanded for the elderly, disabled and sick, which was particularly important as the war had left so many permanently injured people and one-parent families.
- Harsh punishments for being late to, or absent from, work ceased.
- House construction increased so that 108 million people moved into new homes from 1956 to 1965. Much housing was of poor quality but lives changed for millions no longer sharing accommodation.
- The number of doctors, hospitals and students in higher education increased.

However:

- Privileges remained for senior party officials, with access to special health care, holidays and cars.
- Anti-religious propaganda was stepped up and three-quarters of all churches and monasteries, as well as many mosques, were closed down.
- The non-Russian nationalities came under more control from Moscow, with top jobs reserved for Russians.

Cultural change under Khrushchev, 1953–64

With Khrushchev's 'secret speech' came a thaw in cultural life.

- It became easier to access news from the West and, although illegal, many listened to foreign radio stations for news they could trust.
- In 1962, a book called *One Day in the Life of Ivan Denisovich* was published. The author, Aleksandr Solzhenitsyn, had spent eight years in a labour camp, so his fictional account of a day in the life of a prisoner struck a chord (with its stark, honest portrayal of camp life), especially with those recently released. It sold a million copies within six months.
- However, *Dr Zhivago*, by Boris Pasternak, was not passed by the censors as it was critical of the October Revolution. It was published abroad in 1957; the author was awarded the Nobel Prize but not allowed to accept it. It was circulated illegally in the Soviet Union and, when the author died in 1960, thousands attended his funeral.
- The Soviet Union was opened to Western tourists.
- In 1957, Moscow hosted a World Festival of Youth, attended by 34,000 people from 131 countries. One aim was to win over foreign youth to the Soviet way of life. Instead, Soviet youth were won over to jeans and jazz, Western fashion and music, which the foreigners brought with them. These were much more appealing than the conformist culture of Komsomol, the Young Communist organisation.
- Khrushchev was particularly keen to engage young people and reawaken the enthusiasm of the early years of the Revolution. Mobilising hundreds of thousands of youth in the Virgin Lands scheme was the most ambitious scheme he came up with.

Quick quizzes at **www.hoddereducation.co.uk/myrevisionnotes**

Eliminate irrelevance

Below is a sample A-level essay question and a paragraph written in answer to it. Read the paragraph and identify parts that are not directly relevant or helpful to the question. Draw a line through the information that is irrelevant and justify your deletions in the margin.

> 'The living standards of the Soviet people improved consistently in the years 1945–64.' Assess the validity of this view.

In the post-war years, it took many years to rebuild the millions of homes destroyed in the war while the peasantry, in particular, were squeezed, with more grain taken from them. Heavy industry was favoured at the expense of consumer goods, with food and housing being in short supply. Factories and steel works were rebuilt and the production of coal and steel soon reached pre-war levels. This was justified on the grounds that defence and security were priorities. However, living standards rose considerably during the Khrushchev years as he increased spending on the production of food and household goods. He also oversaw a big programme of house-building.

Interpretation question

A full A-level interpretation question consists of three extracts. For this exercise, there are just two extracts. Read each extract in turn and then:

● Identify the main argument and any supplementary arguments put forward.

● Using your own knowledge, explain the arguments and the evidence given in support.

● Evaluate the arguments, pointing out their strengths and shortcomings, and come to a conclusion about how convincing they are.

EXTRACT A

Adapted from O. Figes, Revolutionary Russia, 1891–1991, *page 257 (2015)*

With the renunciation of terror, the regime had to find new ways of popular control and mobilisation. It could no longer count on fear. Seeking to return to the Leninist idea of collective action, Khrushchev attached greater weight to mass participation in policy campaigns and grassroots organisations designed to reawaken the enthusiasm of the Revolution's early years. Among these initiatives were street patrols, which employed millions of volunteers, and house and work committees which were given legal powers to combat 'idlers and social parasites'. But the most ambitious was the 'Virgin Lands' campaign, in which hundreds of thousands of young men and women volunteered to work and settle on the land of Kazakhstan. Invoking Lenin's idea of the NEP, that the international class struggle would be fought out in the economic sphere, Khrushchev stressed the campaign's importance as a visible example of 'the advantages of the socialist over the capitalist system'.

EXTRACT B

Adapted from Martin Sixsmith, Russia: A 1,000-Year Chronicle of the Wild East, *pages 415–16 (2012)*

Khrushchev's goal was to raise Soviet standards of living above those of America, 'to catch up and overtake the United States in per capita production of milk, meat and butter'. Soviet pride was at stake – the target of 'beating the Americans' was intended to boost production in all sectors of the economy. It was a gamble for Khrushchev: as Soviet leader, he had at least a broad grasp of the economic realities and he knew how far Moscow was trailing behind; but his enthusiasm and pugnacity got the better of him. He needed to deliver on his boast. In the early 1960s, he launched a large-scale programme of house-building. Thousands of concrete tower blocks were erected across the country and by the middle of the decade the availability of housing in cities had been greatly improved. However, many of the pre-fabricated multi-storey blocks would need replacing only a few years later and they quickly gained the nickname of khrushcheby – 'Khrushchev's slums'. The economy was slow to respond to Khrushchev's urgings. He had repealed many of Stalin's draconian labour laws: workers could no longer be punished as criminals if they arrived at work more than 20 minutes late. But there were few financial incentives to make people work hard. By 1961, Khrushchev was considering Stalinist methods of coercion.

Opponents of Khrushchev and his fall from power

Cultural dissidents

The 'thaw' allowed for more artistic and intellectual freedom and a new group of 'cultural dissidents' emerged. Most were keen to promote human rights and greater democracy because the Soviet Union was still a highly authoritarian state with a network of spies and informers. The written word, in particular, was a way of expressing political views, either through works published abroad and then smuggled into the country or through *samizdat*. This practice entailed the rewriting and retyping of articles, poems and books which were then distributed through personal contacts. It became a genuine underground press, spreading information and opinion on Soviet politics and society. Several writers were imprisoned for criticising the regime and thousands more were condemned for their 'anti-social, parasitic way of life'. There was also an 'underground' music scene, with tapes of jazz, rock 'n' roll and Western pop music circulated.

Opposition within the party

Many party colleagues never forgave Khrushchev for his 'secret speech'. In particular, the hardliners, like Molotov, felt that the speech undermined the unity and authority of the party. In 1957, the hardliners tried to force Khrushchev from power. They secured majority support in the Presidium but Khrushchev appealed to the Central Committee, the larger body, and he also had the support of the army and KGB. He survived. His opponents were sent a long way from Moscow, to insignificant jobs, but they were not executed.

On Khrushchev's 70th birthday, in April 1964, his deputy, **Leonid Brezhnev**, praised Khrushchev for his achievements. However, a few months later, Brezhnev led the opposition, which now included Khrushchev's former supporters, in both the Presidium and the Central Committee, and forced Khrushchev to resign. At first, it was announced that Khrushchev had resigned because of 'age and ill health'. Later, the press denounced him for his 'hare-brained schemes, half-baked conclusions, hasty decisions'. Khrushchev was given a flat in Moscow, a house in the country, a car and a pension, although he was officially ignored. However, there was no purge, except of his son-in-law, who had been given wide-ranging powers by Khrushchev.

Reasons for Khrushchev's fall from power

- By 1964, Khrushchev had aroused the resentment of many different groups.
- There was criticism of his 'one-man style' of ruling, his arrogance and failure to take advice.
- Failure of his Virgin Lands scheme led to a shortfall in food supplies so that grain had to be imported from the USA and Canada.
- His decentralisation of economic controls caused anger among party leaders in Moscow.
- His promotion of consumer goods upset those who wanted continued emphasis on heavy industry.
- The military disliked his focus on building nuclear missiles at the expense of conventional weapons.
- There were an increasing number of protests and strikes by workers, especially after a rise in food prices in 1962.
- There was criticism of his foreign policy.
- He promoted and gave much power to his son-in-law.

How far do you agree?

Read the following interpretation on the reasons for Khrushchev's fall from power. Summarise the main arguments and then add your own knowledge to agree with or contradict each of the arguments.

EXTRACT A

Adapted from John Gooding, Rulers and Subjects: Government and People in Russia, 1801–1991, *page 239 (1996)*

Toppling a Soviet leader was unprecedented, but there were two reasons why by 1964 his colleagues wanted very badly to get rid of Khrushchev. First, there was his attack on Stalin. The attack had, admittedly, been on Stalin rather than on Stalinism: on terror and arbitrariness rather than on the fundamental structures of the Stalinist state. Any such attack was, however, dangerous. Once the party had been shown to be guilty, directly or indirectly, of wrongdoing, even in a limited area, then its claim to infallibility, its mystique, and the justification for its monopoly of power were in jeopardy. People might suspect an underlying flaw in the system. Second, there was Khrushchev's Bolshevism – his 'back to Lenin' emphasis. As a piece of public relations, 'back to Lenin' was fine. But Khrushchev had turned out to be a Bolshevik idealist with something of the naivety and impetuosity of the 1920s. Communism for him was not merely a distant goal which gave the party legitimacy and a purpose but something to be achieved in the very near future. To be exact, it would be achieved during the 1980s, by which time the Soviet Union would have overtaken the USA in its living standards. Yet Khrushchev's promises were extremely hazardous for the party. The timetable was unrealistic, indeed positively reckless. The trouble was that the great economic advance of the 1950s was showing distinct signs of faltering by the early 1960s. Boasts about communism and overtaking the Americans had begun to look foolish.

Developing an argument

Below is a sample exam question, a list of key points to be made in the essay and a paragraph from the essay. Read the question, the plan and the sample paragraph. Rewrite the paragraph in order to develop an argument. Your paragraph should answer the question directly and set out the evidence that supports your argument. Crucially, it should develop an argument by setting out a general answer to the question and reasons that support this.

'The use of terror enabled Stalin to rule the Soviet Union until his death. Khrushchev's failure to exploit terror explains why he was ousted in 1964.' Assess the validity of this view.

Key points:

- Stalin outmanoeuvred colleagues on his way to establishing a personal dictatorship.
- He used terror, especially the secret police, to eliminate opposition and the 'cult of personality' to win mass support.
- Khrushchev dismantled Stalin's dictatorship and did not use terror as Stalin had done.
- His colleagues decided to oust Khrushchev and he gave in to their pressure.

Sample paragraph

Stalin established a personal dictatorship and eliminated opposition by the use of terror. He also used the cult of personality to win mass support and was portrayed as a father figure. Khrushchev revealed the extent of Stalin's brutality, dismantled his dictatorship and did not use terror. He was ousted because his colleagues plotted his downfall while he was on holiday. He accepted their decision, rather than resorting to terror to oppose them.

The political, economic and social condition of the Soviet Union by 1964

The political situation

Khrushchev had decided not to fight against his colleagues when they demanded his resignation in 1964. He said to them: 'Could anyone have dreamt of telling Stalin that he didn't suit us anymore, and suggesting that he retire? He would have annihilated them. Everything is different now. The fear has gone; we can talk as equals. That is my contribution.' It is certainly a fitting epitaph: Khrushchev left his country freer, happier and more prosperous. Society was more open and less fearful. Millions of prisoners had been released from the labour camps. By 1964, mass terror had ended and less use was made of the state's powers of coercion.

The Soviet Union was never the same again after Khrushchev's 'secret speech'. There would never be a return to the mass terror of the Stalin years. Khrushchev's speech had shaken up the Soviet Union but, once the dust had settled, the country became more stable than at any time over the previous hundred years. Most people were more content too.

However, although the Soviet Union was no longer an autocracy, as it had been under Stalin, it remained a one-party state. The political elite had risen to power under Stalin and they were never going to relinquish their control over the state. Their lives, their careers and the accompanying privileges depended on it.

The economic and social situation

With the disappearance of terror as a method of government, there was more emphasis on improving the material conditions of the people in order to maintain support for the government and to show that Soviet socialism worked. For instance, in the early 1960s, the military budget was cut to pay for food imports and a big housing programme. The Soviet Union became a more consumer-based economy with much improved living standards (even if lower than those in the USA and Western Europe).

The economy was still subject to a high degree of central planning and this was not conducive to initiative and innovation. Khrushchev made an increase in agricultural productivity his priority yet there was no significant increase in the output of farms or factories by 1964. Agriculture remained backward and many young people continued to leave the villages for the city. The Soviet Union was a far more urban than rural society by 1964. Women formed the backbone of the rural economy. However, developments in military and space technology were highly impressive and Khrushchev was instrumental in this success. The Soviet Union maintained its reputation as a great military power.

Censorship was tightened in the 1960s, following the years of the 'thaw', and *samizdat* publishing increased. Overall, however, Khrushchev had relaxed the rigid controls on cultural life during his years in power and there was an undoubted flowering of Russian art and culture by 1964.

Develop the detail

Below is a sample A-level exam question, followed by a series of statements to be used in an answer. Add relevant, specific detail to each of the statements in order to increase the value of the answer.

'In the years 1945–53, the economy was stagnant. Under Khrushchev, it grew.' To what extent do you agree with this view?

- The economy was not stagnant from 1945 to 1953. However, the production of consumer goods was neglected.
- Grain exports, to pay for spending on industry and technology, were increased from 1945 to 1953.
- There was a growth in the production of consumer goods and housing under Khrushchev.
- There was much investment in food production after 1953.
- The economy grew in the late 1950s but growth slowed down in the early 1960s.

Turning assertion into argument

Below is a series of definitions, a sample A-level exam question and two sample conclusions. One of the conclusions achieves a high mark because it contains an argument. The other achieves a lower mark because it contains only description and assertion. Identify which is which. The mark scheme on page 7 will help you.

Description: a detailed account

Assertion: a statement of fact or an opinion which is not supported by a reason

Reason: a statement which explains or justifies something

Argument: an assertion justified with a reason.

To what extent was the Soviet Union politically transformed in the years 1945 to 1963?

Overall, the Soviet Union was transformed. Stalin was a dictator. He had his opponents executed, even if less frequently after the 1930s, and he was worshipped like a Tsar. He was portrayed as a genius and his birthday was a day of major celebration. After his death, millions of prisoners were released and Khrushchev made the 'secret speech', which explained how Stalin had used terror to rule. Khrushchev was not a dictator and he did not have his opponents executed. Also, he resigned in 1964 rather than use force to get rid of his opponents. The Soviet Union was no longer ruled by terror.

In conclusion, Stalin remained in dictatorial control until his death in 1953. He continued to exercise a personal dictatorship and made extensive use of the secret police in order to remove actual and imagined opponents. Then, after 1953, a collective leadership emerged and over a million prisoners were released. Censorship was eased and the powers of the secret police were reduced. No longer would the country be ruled by a personal dictatorship reliant on terror. Even when Khrushchev emerged as leader, he continued to attack Stalinism and to release millions of political prisoners. Khrushchev's enforced resignation in 1964 was carried out peacefully. Soviet citizens remained more free than they had been under Stalin and lived more secure, happy lives. However, most of the personnel who had come to power under Stalin remained in post and the Soviet Union remained a one-party state with a network of spies and informers.

Exam focus (A-level)

REVISED

Below is a sample Level 5 answer on interpretations. It was written in response to an A-level question.

Using your understanding of the historical context, assess how convincing the arguments in these three extracts are in relation to Soviet rule under Khrushchev.

EXTRACT A

Adapted from Edward Acton, Russia – The Tsarist and Soviet Legacy *(1995)*

The post-Stalin generation saw Russia become more stable than at any time since the days of Alexander I [1801–25]. The recipe for this stability was based upon two key ingredients. The first was a marked and general improvement in the standard of living. The second was the paradoxical combination of military might and chronic national insecurity which was Stalin's legacy. Both were exploited to the full to rally mass support behind the Soviet system. Despite the slackening of censorship and cultural control which accompanied 'destalinisation', the Party did all it could to ensure that, from cradle to grave, every citizen was convinced that both material progress and peace depended on 'Soviet socialism'.

EXTRACT B

Adapted from D. Volkogonov, The Rise and Fall of the Soviet Empire *(1999)*

Khrushchev sensed that he had right on his side. This sense became stronger after he got rid of his main rivals and was able to implement numerous reforms in the stagnant country. The ossified state and society, mired in bureaucracy and dogmatism, adapted poorly to the cascade of change, yet the country did break free of its former anchorage. The decade of Khrushchev's rule demonstrated his potential as an innovator, a demolition artist, experimenter, opportunist and inventor. It was if he had suddenly woken up. Initiatives followed one after the other ... [However,] Khrushchev's endless proposals and new regulations produced very little in the way of positive results. Nor could they, as long as it was not realised that the capacity of the Leninist system for reform was extremely limited. The people became disgruntled and jokes about 'Nikita' [his first name] proliferated. His courageous speech at the Twentieth Congress had given the population a taste of freedom, and they wanted more, but he had not wanted to alter the basic form of the system or the economic foundations of the country.

EXTRACT C

Adapted from J. P. Nettl, The Soviet Achievement *(1967)*

Khrushchev represented the wishes and sentiments of the Soviet population and particularly of the Party. The new contract with the outside world, even with the arch-imperialist United States, was genuinely welcomed everywhere. The doctrine of peaceful co-existence, according to which communism would succeed by demonstration of superiority instead of revolutionary or military destruction of its opponents, was only a theoretical justification for the determination of the newly educated and professional groups in positions of power not to live any longer in an inbred, isolated world of their own. The incessant call for reform and modernisation, for the exploitation of the enormous industrial potential of the Soviet Union, struck a deep chord among all these groups. Above all, the self-confident articulation of Soviet power challenging American technological and political domination contrasted favourably with the fearful and defensive isolationism of Stalin. In all these directions Khrushchev represented the future, and had the support of the most progressive groups in Soviet society.

Extract A argues that Russia became more stable in the years after Stalin despite 'destalinisation' and the accompanying 'slackening' of government control of public opinion. It argues that this increased stability was based on two key features. The first was an improved standard of living. Certainly, during Khrushchev's years in power, there were huge improvements made in food supplies, housing, education and the provision of household goods. The second feature identified in the extract is the combination of military strength and national insecurity which was inherited from Stalin. The government repeatedly impressed upon the people that they were now better off, which was increasingly important now that citizens were no longer terrorised into silent, uncomplaining submission as they had been under Stalin. The extract also explains how, in order to enhance this stability, the new government followed Stalin in stressing the country's military might, which kept them safe, and, paradoxically, its insecurity. The latter was emphasised in order to justify huge military expenditure and to assure the people that the government was doing all it could to counter the threat of its enemies, particularly of the USA. In these ways, the government strove to convince its people that, 'from cradle to grave', they could feel safe and secure in the knowledge that 'Soviet socialism' was ensuring 'both material progress and peace'. This extract is highly convincing as an explanation of the undoubted stability which Khrushchev, as the most significant of 'Stalin's successors', brought to the Soviet Union during his years in power. It might have added that the Soviet Union remained a highly authoritarian, one-party state, with a network of spies and informers which, alongside the huge material advances mentioned, ensured a high degree of conformism and, thus, stability.

This paragraph identifies and corroborates the main arguments with appropriate supporting evidence and concludes with sound critical comment.

Extract B argues that Khrushchev's sense of conviction enabled him to 'implement numerous reforms'. This change, it argues, was particularly necessary because the Soviet Union had become highly bureaucratic, dogmatic, even 'stagnant', and that Khrushchev was successful in enabling the country to make a break from the past. It implies that, overnight, Khrushchev revealed that he could innovate, experiment, demolish and invent. However, his cascade of initiatives often bore little fruit, partly because, although he wished for a return to the revolutionary spirit of the 1920s, he did not succeed in liberating the government from the constraints of the 'Leninist system'. In fact, Khrushchev did not wish to alter the basis of that system and thus his reforms were limited. So, although Khrushchev had whetted the popular appetite for reform with his secret speech, he did not satisfy it. This led people to become 'disgruntled' and to poke fun at him. This extract highlights, very effectively, the limited nature of reform which Khrushchev implemented. In explanation, it might have added that he was severely constrained by the fact that most of the elite, like him, had come to power during, and benefited from, Stalin's rule and would most probably have ousted him rather than allow him to carry out more radical reform.

This paragraph clearly and closely elucidates the main arguments with some good evaluation and an apt contrast with Extract A.

Extract C argues that Khrushchev's modernising, forward-looking approach reflected the wishes of the people and party, particularly of the 'newly educated and professional groups', who appreciated the more open, outward-looking attitude represented by the doctrine of peaceful co-existence. These groups particularly responded to Khrushchev's 'self-confident articulation of Soviet power', which would be demonstrated by the exploitation of the Soviet Union's industrial potential and the accompanying rise in living standards. These developments, together with advances in rocketry and space exploration, would then enable the Soviet Union to catch up with, even overtake, the Americans both economically and technologically. This, in the eyes of 'the most progressive groups in Soviet society', represented the future and a complete break from the 'fearful, defensive isolationism' of the Stalin years. This extract offers a convincing explanation of why so many, especially in the elites, supported Khrushchev. It implies that, by identifying and reflecting the wishes of so many, Khrushchev was able to gain widespread support and thus make the Soviet Union more stable. However, it makes no mention of the fact that many of the elites were to become frustrated, even resentful, of changes that seemed to involve more meddling than substantial improvement.

This paragraph highlights the key arguments with use of well-selected quotations from the extract. Appropriate contextual knowledge is used in support of the arguments and the final sentence identifies evidence to counter the main argument.

This is a highly effective answer which provides thorough corroboration of the main arguments in each extract. It weaves in contextual knowledge to support, and also to challenge, the arguments and makes some apt inferences. It provides good, comparative evaluation of the extracts.

Find the evidence

The most important element in analysing and evaluating an argument is supporting evidence and examples. Read the answer again and identify where evidence has been used effectively to support a point.

Glossary

Anti-Semitism   Prejudice or hatred towards the Jews.

Autocracy   The possession of total power by one person; the ruler's word is law.

Bolshevik Party   Led by Lenin, this faction broke away from the Social Democratic Workers' Party in 1903. It seized power in Russia in October 1917.

Bureaucrats   Civil servants who undertake administrative tasks.

Burzhui   A term of abuse used against anyone who seemed well off or anti-communist.

Central Committee   A body elected by the party congress.

Cheka   The Bolshevik secret police.

Civil rights   Personal rights, for example freedom of speech, movement and religion.

Cold War   The tension between the Soviet Union and the USA after the Second World War.

Commissars   Socialist government ministers.

Conscription   Forced service, for example in the army.

Constituent assembly   A governing body that will draw up a new constitution.

Constitutional monarchy   A monarchy in which the ruler's power is limited by an elected assembly.

Crimean War   A war in 1853–56 in which the British and French fought on Turkey's behalf against Russia.

Dual authority/Dual power   A power-sharing arrangement in 1917 between the Provisional Government and the Petrograd Soviet.

Duma   The Russian term for an elected governing assembly.

Emancipation   Freedom; in the Russian context, this often refers to the edict which gave the serfs their freedom.

Ethnic or national minorities   People of different ethnic or national backgrounds, such as Poles, Finns, Ukrainians and Jews, who lived within the state of Imperial Russia and later the Soviet Union.

Import tariffs   Monetary duties paid to the state when goods are brought into a country.

Intelligentsia/Intellectuals   The educated upper-class or middle-class elites who were often critical of the Tsarist regime.

Kadets   Members of the Constitutional Democratic Party, who accepted the October Manifesto (1905).

Kolkhoz   A collective farm.

Komsomol   The Young Communist organisation.

Kronstadt   St Petersburg's main seaport.

Kulaks   Wealthy peasant farmers who owned land and employed labour.

Land Captains   Noble officials with extensive local powers, including the right to overrule the local Zemstva.

Land and Liberty   An organisation derived from the Populist belief that land should be divided between the peasants.

Liberals   Those wanting more personal and economic freedom. This term was often applied to those in favour of representative, elected government.

Mandate   The authority to carry out a policy.

Marxism   A political ideology derived from the theories of Karl Marx, who taught that all history is driven by economic forces which, in turn, create class struggles.

Menshevik Party   A Marxist party that split from the Bolsheviks in 1903.

Mir   A Russian village commune where the peasants lived and worked.

Mortgage   Borrowing money against some form of security, such as property.

Narodnik   The Russian name for a populist, someone who believes in the power of the people.

NKVD   The secret police that succeeded the Cheka.

Nomenklatura   A privileged elite of officials who ran the party machine.

Octobrists   A moderate conservative party, supported by landowners and industrialists, that accepted the October Manifesto.

Okhrana   The Tsarist secret police force which replaced the Third Section in 1880.

Orthodox Church   The official state religion of Tsarist Russia.

Pogrom   An attack on Jews – often accompanied by arson, raping and looting.

Politburo   The highest policy-making body in the Soviet Union.

Proletarian A member of the exploited industrial working class.

Provisional Government The government that ruled the Russian Empire on a temporary basis after the fall of the Tsar. The Provisional Government was deposed by Lenin's October Revolution.

Purge Literally 'a cleaning out of impurities'. In practice, Stalin's terror tactic for getting rid of his enemies.

Radical 'Radix' is the Latin word for 'root', hence radical change is fundamental change – from the roots.

Reaction Backward-looking behaviour which meant returning to former (conservative) ways.

Red Guards Bolshevik armed forces.

Russification The practice of imposing Russian language and culture on national minority groups while repressing their own ethnicities.

Samizdat Secret publication of banned literature.

Serfdom A social system in which legally 'bound' peasants are the property of their landlords.

Serfs Agricultural labourers who are the personal property of their masters and can be bought and sold.

Show trials Propagandist trials held in front of an audience for a political purpose.

Slavophiles Members of the Russian intelligentsia who believed Russia should seek a basis for its future development in its native traditions and not follow the Western model.

Socialist Someone who believes in socialism – that factories and land should belong to the people.

Social Democratic Workers' Party A Marxist Party founded in 1898. In 1903, it split into the two factions: the Bolsheviks and the Mensheviks.

Socialist Revolutionary Party A party built on populism, founded in 1901. It supported land redistribution among peasants. It advocated terrorist methods, including assassination.

Soviet An elected council, usually of workers, soldiers, sailors and perhaps peasants, which controlled a factory or a local area. A soviet was set up in St Petersburg in 1905.

Sovnarkom The Soviet Council of People's Commissars, a committee which led Lenin's government after the October Revolution.

Stakhanovite A movement named after a miner who broke all records with the amount of coal he mined in one shift, in 1935.

St Petersburg The capital of Russia (known as Petrograd from 1914 and later Leningrad).

Trade unions Organisations which represent workers in negotiations with employers. Before 1905, these were illegal in Russia.

Tsar The title given to the Emperor of Russia. It derives from the Latin word 'Caesar' and means 'Emperor'.

Universal suffrage The vote for all adults; in the nineteenth century, this usually meant the vote for all men.

War credits Special loans granted in wartime.

Westernisers Members of the Russian intelligentsia who believed Russia should develop along the lines followed by Western nations.

Winter Palace The home of the Tsar in the centre of St Petersburg (Petrograd).

Zemstva Elected local government assemblies set up in Russia in 1864.

Key figures

Alexander II Ruled as Tsar from 1855 to 1881. He is sometimes known as the 'Tsar Liberator', primarily for his abolition of serfdom and other reforms. Assassinated in 1881.

Alexander III Succeeded his father in 1881. He opposed his father's reforming policies and repressed political opposition.

Alexandra The German wife of Nicholas II.

Beria, Lavrenty Head of the NKVD from 1938. He was executed in 1953.

Brezhnev, Leonid A close ally of Khrushchev; he eventually led the group that forced him from power.

Father Gapon An Orthodox priest who organised workers' unions from 1903 but remained loyal to the Tsar. He fled into exile after Bloody Sunday but was later hanged.

Kamenev, Lev An active Bolshevik from 1905 and later a member of the Politburo. He was executed in the purges of 1936.

Kerensky, Alexander A Socialist Revolutionary who sat in the Petrograd Soviet and Provisional Government in 1917, rising to become leader of that government from July. He was deposed by the Bolsheviks in October.

Khrushchev, Nikita First Secretary of the party from 1953 to 1964 who had emerged as leader in the mid-1950s. He delivered the 'secret speech' in 1956, which revealed the extent of Stalin's purges. He was ousted in 1964.

Kirov, Sergei A popular figure, he was Party Secretary in Leningrad before being assassinated in 1934.

Kornilov, Lavr Army general who attempted a coup against the Provisional Government in August 1917.

Lavrov, Peter A populist who, in 1874, led a group of students into the countryside to live, and spread their ideas, among the peasants.

Lenin, Vladimir Leader of the Bolsheviks from 1903, he shaped the communist state which emerged after the 1917 October Revolution. He died in 1924 and the city of Petrograd was renamed 'Leningrad' after him.

Malenkov, Georgy Prime Minister and leading reformer after Stalin's death, he was forced to resign by Khrushchev in 1955.

Martov, Julius A leader of the Social Democratic Workers' Party, he broke with Lenin and led the Mensheviks.

Milyutin, Nicholas and Dmitri Two brothers who were both close advisers of Nicholas II.

Molotov, Vyacheslav Served under Stalin and was part of the collective leadership that ruled the Soviet Union after Stalin's death.

Nicholas II Tsar from 1894 until his abdication in February 1917. Determined to uphold the Tsarist autocracy, he proved to be an indecisive ruler.

Pobedonostev, Konstantin Tutor to Alexander III and later to Nicholas II, he encouraged Alexander to maintain highly autocratic government.

Prince Lvov A wealthy aristocratic landowner who had led the Kadets and Russian Union of Zemstva before becoming leader of the Provisional Government in 1917.

Rasputin, Gregory A mystic peasant who exercised great influence with the Empress Alexandra and then in the Tsarist government in the early years of the First World War. He was assassinated in 1916.

Stalin, Joseph General Secretary of the Communist Party from 1922, he exercised increasingly dictatorial control over the Soviet Union until his death in 1953.

Stolypin, Peter Interior Minister from 1906 to 1911, he introduced major reforms in agriculture but was assassinated in 1911.

Trotsky, Leon A brilliant orator, he masterminded the takeover of Petrograd by Red Guards in October 1917 and the Bolshevik victory in the Civil War. He was assassinated on Stalin's orders in Mexico in 1940.

Von Reutern, Mikhail Minister of Finance under Alexander II from 1862 to 1878.

Vyshnegradsky, Ivan Finance Minister from 1887 to 1892.

Witte, Sergei Finance Minister from 1892 to 1903; he is credited with the rapid expansion of the Russian economy at the end of the nineteenth and early twentieth century.

Zinoviev, Gregory A close ally of Lenin, he played a prominent part in the October Revolution but was purged by Stalin in 1936.

Timeline

1855	Alexander II becomes Tsar
1861	Abolition of serfdom
1874	Populists begin campaign to 'Go to the People'
1881	Assassination of Alexander II
1891–2	Widespread famine
1892–1903	Sergei Witte is Minister of Finance – rapid industrialisation programme
1894	Death of Alexander III; accession of Nicholas II
1898	Foundation of Russian Social Democratic Workers' Party (SDs)
1901–5	Agrarian and industrial unrest
1903	Split of SDs into Bolsheviks (led by Lenin) and Mensheviks (led by Martov)
1904	War breaks out between Russia and Japan
1905	January – 'Bloody Sunday' massacre leads to revolutionary upheavals
	October – October Manifesto authorises elections to a State Duma; the St Petersburg Soviet is formed
1906–11	Stolypin carries through programme of agrarian reform
1912	Lena goldfields massacre – renewed industrial unrest
1914	1 August – Germany declares war on Russia
1915	6 September – Tsar assumes command of the armed forces and suspends the Duma
1917	February – Strikes and civil unrest in Petrograd
	27 February – Troops refuse to fire on demonstrators and join the revolutionary movement; formation of the Petrograd Soviet
	March – First Provisional Government is formed; Tsar abdicates
	July – Anti-government demonstrations – the 'July Days' and Kornilov's attempted coup

	24–25 October – Bolsheviks seize key buildings in Petrograd
	25–27 October – Provisional Government members are arrested; Bolshevik government announced; decrees on peace and land
	December – Establishment of the Cheka
1918	January – Constituent Assembly forcibly dissolved
	Start of Civil War
1921	New Economic Policy
1924	Death of Lenin
1928	First Five-Year Plan
1929	Start of mass collectivisation and call for liquidation of kulaks
1932–33	Famine in Ukraine and elsewhere.
1936	Show trial of Zinoviev, Kamenev and others
1937–38	Height of Great Terror
1941	Nazi invasion of Soviet Union; siege of Leningrad begins
1942	Battle of Stalingrad
1945	End of Second World War
1949	Leningrad Affair
1952	Doctors' plot
1953	Death of Stalin
1954	Start of Khrushchev's 'Virgin Lands' scheme
1956	Khrushchev's 'secret speech' and de-Stalinisation
1958	Pasternak awarded Nobel Prize for Dr Zhivago
1962	Publication of Solzhenitsyn's One Day in the Life of Ivan Denisovich
1964	Removal of Khrushchev

Quick quizzes at **www.hoddereducation.co.uk/myrevisionnotes**

Answers

Section 1: Trying to preserve autocracy, 1855–94

Page 9, Summarise the arguments

Russia was too undeveloped to remain a great power. She had lost the Crimean War because she lacked modern railways and weaponry. Russian society, as a whole, needed to learn from Western Europe in order to become more modern and, thus, powerful.

Page 9, Identify an argument

Answer 2 contains the argument; answer 1 is descriptive.

Page 11, Complete the paragraph

Insert the following after the first sentence:

Certainly the first two years were little different since the freed serfs had to perform two years of labour service before they became free. Even after this, however, the former serfs were required to make redemption payments for the land they were given and until these were paid, they had to remain in their mir. This effectively condemned them to a lifestyle that was little different from that they had previously known. Furthermore, the land was often overpriced by corrupt local landowning officials, leaving the former serfs in considerable debt, while allocations varied and could be inadequate. Without the use of the meadows, pasture and woodland, which went to the landowners, some peasants had barely enough to live on.

Page 11, Interpretation: content or argument?

The second answer focuses more on the arguments.

Page 13, Delete as applicable

Select '**just one of many reasons**' and later '**was connected with**' and then follow as below:

This is because it was no longer possible to ignore the rights of the freed peasants. However, the military reforms were as much the result of the catastrophes of the Crimean War and the liberal thinking of the Milyutin brothers as the product of emancipation. Similarly, the reasons for the local government and judicial reforms can be said to have been the demands of the intelligentsia and the Tsar's own concerns that Russia should catch up with the West. Since the peasants had limited representation on the Zemstva and still had their own courts, it cannot be said that either of these measures was primarily designed to serve or respond to peasant needs.

Page 13, Eliminate irrelevance

Among the reforms that transformed Russian society were changes in education. The changes were introduced by Alexander II's Education Minister, Golovnin, who, like the Milyutin brothers, had liberal ideas. The educational changes came to an end when Golovnin was replaced by the conservative Tolstoy in 1866. In 1864, the new Zemstva were given responsibility for the provision of education in their own areas. These Zemstva were elected councils chosen by the nobles, townspeople, Church and peasants, although voting was arranged in a way that allowed the nobles more influence. The schools they established were made available to all, which helped transform society, even though the poor rarely got beyond primary level. Although the serfs had been emancipated in 1861, many were still very poor and reliant on subsistence farming. The educational curriculum was also expanded, with new scientific subjects and vocational secondary schools offering opportunities for advancement. There was still a very small middle class in Russia though. The universities were given more control over the courses they offered. This transformed society by creating a new group of critical and radical students.

Page 15, Turning assertion into argument

... because they promoted the growth of the legal profession, which attracted young, educated and critical middle-class intellectuals and provided juries with a chance to show their sympathies when faced with cases involving anti-Tsarist activities.

... so allowing the works of radical socialist thinkers, such as Nikolai Chernyshevsky, Alexander Herzen and Mikhail Bakunin, to spread.

... because the reforms gave the universities greater independence to teach the subjects they wished to and employ whomsoever they wanted, as well as ensuring there was a larger student body which became receptive to new thinking.

Page 17, Spot the mistake

There is no attempt to assess whether the opposition, such as that of the Narodniks and Black Partition, had any success at all.

Page 19, How far do you agree?

Alexander III wanted to unify his empire by making it emphatically Russian. He forced the Russian language on non-Russian speaking minorities. He intended to unite his country but his policy intensified national feeling.

He was so afraid of opposition that he was quick to restrict freedoms. He had many members of People's Will arrested and made increased use of the Okhrana and secret trials.

Revolutionary activity was driven underground, not eliminated. Hence, he made more use of spies.

Page 21, Summarise the arguments

Many households were divided after emancipation and were thus left with less livestock and equipment. The peasantry's egalitarianism meant that they had little incentive to be productive except in babies. This led to land shortage and growing landlessness. Agriculture remained less mechanised and intensive.

Page 21, Support or challenge?

1	Support	3	Challenge	5	Challenge
2	Challenge	4	Support	6	Support

Section 2: The collapse of autocracy, 1894–1917

Page 27, Introducing and concluding an argument

In the introduction, it would be worth giving an example of a factor that was not the government's responsibility, such as land hunger or harsh working and living conditions in the cities.

In conclusion, you could mention the personal shortcomings of Nicholas II as a Tsar.

Page 29, Use own knowledge to support or contradict

Main argument: Nicholas II was so opposed to any limitation on his autocratic powers that he failed to pass even moderate reform.

Counter-argument: Nicholas II did agree, or so it appeared, to become a constitutional monarch in his October Manifesto but he had no intention of doing so, as shown in the 'Fundamental Laws'.

Page 31, Turning assertion into argument

... A new rouble, backed by gold, was introduced in 1897 and it increased business confidence.

... By 1914, Russia had over 60,000 kilometres of railway track which, in turn, stimulated the development of the coal, iron and steel industries.

... However, this made Russian industry highly dependent on this source of finance and thus vulnerable because it could dry up at any time.

... These allowed peasants to consolidate their land and buy it from the mir, encouraging the growth of a new, more efficient class of peasant, the kulak. By 1909, Russia was the world's leading exporter of cereals.

... This made the peasants reluctant to change their farming methods. Furthermore, there was an acute land shortage.

Page 31, Develop the detail

Between 1894 and 1914, Russia experienced massive industrial growth. By 1914, it had a huge railway network and had vastly increased its production of coal, iron and oil: production of the latter three trebled over the 20 years. However, its economic expansion started from a low base compared with the economies of Western Europe and the USA and was highly dependent on foreign investment, which could be withdrawn at any time. Agriculture also experienced considerable development so that, by 1914, Russia had become the world's leading exporter of cereals. The kulak class of peasants formed a more efficient and profitable sector of the rural economy but most agriculture was still based on traditional and inefficient methods so that Russian agriculture as a whole was far less productive than that of Western Europe and the USA. Between 1894 and 1914, Russia became economically stronger, especially in heavy industry, but much of its agriculture remained undeveloped.

Page 33, Spot the mistake

While rightly stressing the instability of the years 1912–14, it should be acknowledged that there was massive support for the Tsar shown in the Romanov tercentenary celebrations of 1913, while the outbreak of war in 1914 rallied patriotic feeling across the classes.

Page 33, Complete the paragraph

... As the urban population increased, many lived and worked in crowded, insanitary conditions. Some were forced to sleep by their machines in the factories. Many houses in St Petersburg had no running water.

Page 35, Use own knowledge to support or contradict

Main argument: More land was cultivated and farming methods improved so that yields rose and consumption increased.

Counter-argument: The gulf between the kulaks and the poorest, landless peasants widened and living standards varied enormously between regions.

Page 35, Developing an argument

There was much change in the cities, even if less in the countryside. The urban population more than doubled in size from 1894 to 1914 so that factory workers made up ten per cent of the population by 1914. There was a huge increase in labour militancy, culminating in a rash of strikes from 1912 to 1914. There was considerable emigration from the countryside but pressure on land intensified because of the fast-rising population. Although a small class of kulaks emerged, most peasants stayed loyal to the mir and maintained traditional farming practices. They also remained loyal to the Tsar and the Church.

Page 37, Support or challenge?

1	Challenge	4	Challenge
2	Support	5	Support
3	Support	6	Support

Page 37, Eliminate irrelevance

The sentence: 'He appointed Stolypin, whose "necktie" suppressed rural unrest and forced the leaders of the St Petersburg Soviet into exile' can be eliminated as it is not relevant to a question about the Tsar and the liberal opposition.

Page 39, Delete as applicable

The demands of opposition movements were **not a particularly major threat** to the Tsarist governments in the years 1881–1914. The liberal intelligentsia's desire for a constitutional monarchy **did not weaken** the Tsarist autocracy. The aims of the radical opposition were highly revolutionary but, in practice, it was **less of a threat**. This was because it was divided between the Socialist Revolutionaries and Social Democrats and also because, in 1905, the St Petersburg Soviet was suppressed and its leader, Trotsky, exiled while Lenin fled abroad. The liberal opposition was largely won over by the October Manifesto and, although it was frustrated by the Tsar's subsequent treatment of the Dumas, it did not weaken the power of the regime.

Page 39, Interpretation: content or argument?

The second answer contains far more argument.

Page 41, Summarise the arguments

Despite increasing social unrest, the Tsar refused to concede any reform to the liberal opposition. In this stance, he was supported by the military leadership, industrialists and nobles.

Page 43, How far do you agree?

Main argument: Acute hardship in St Petersburg created the popular feeling that ordinary people would continue to suffer unless the Tsarist regime was overthrown. Instead of being seen as a protector of his people, the Tsar came to be seen as having betrayed his people, and was increasingly hated, especially after 1905.

Supporting evidence: The demands of the war contributed to increasing hunger and desperation in the capital. These, in turn, led to huge strikes and demonstrations which increasingly called for the abdication of the Tsar. Nicholas II ordered troops to suppress the unrest but the garrison mutinied and joined the protesters. As a result, the Tsar lost control of St Petersburg and three days later, he abdicated.

Page 43, Develop the detail

... He had refused to make concessions to the liberal opposition until 1905 and, then after issuing the October Manifesto, he had gone back on his word and refused to co-operate with the Duma.

... Millions of soldiers went into battle ill-equipped and were subsequently killed, wounded or taken prisoner.

... The generals had little faith in Nicholas as commander-in-chief and the ministers became increasingly disillusioned with a government dominated by the German-born Alexandra and Rasputin.

... Many of the soldiers joined those who were protesting against the government.

Page 47, Interpretation: content or argument?

The second answer contains more argument.

Page 47, Introducing and concluding an argument

Introduction: This would be improved by pointing out that Lenin's treatment of the Constituent Assembly was more autocratic than the Tsar's dissolution of the Duma in 1906 because the Tsar did at least allow several more Dumas to be elected.

Conclusion: This would be improved if it read: 'In conclusion, in January 1918, Russia had a government that was just as autocratic as it had been under Tsar Nicholas II, if not more so.

Section 3: The emergence of communist dictatorship, 1917–41

Page 55, Use own knowledge to support or contradict

Interpretation offered by the extract: The Bolshevik Party and state were created by Lenin and both were shaped by him.

Counter-argument: Others played significant parts both before and after 1917. Trotsky was prominent in the Civil War and Stalin, especially as General Secretary of the Communist Party from 1922, had huge influence over the development of the party.

Page 57, Turning assertion into argument

... They used similar methods although the Cheka was more ruthless.

... Nicholas II's 'Fundamental Laws' rendered the Duma pretty ineffectual although it could and did continue to criticise the Tsar's government, whereas the closing of the Constituent Assembly ended any semblance of representative government in Communist government.

... Many Russians revered the Tsar as semi-divine, whereas Lenin was only made the object of a personality cult after his death.

... Before 1917, Russian industry was privately owned even if dependent on government, especially in securing foreign loans, whereas after 1917, the state took control of most heavy industry.

Page 57, Develop the detail

... The government's failure contributed to military defeat.

... They used the Cheka and army units to do this.

... They gave these essential workers priority over their 'enemies' in the bourgeoisie.

... They were unsuccessful and their actions contributed to revolution.

... This helped to ensure that the production of weapons was sustained.

Page 59, Interpretation: content or argument?

The first answer largely focuses on the content but the second makes inferences and is more analytical.

Page 63, Introducing and concluding an argument

Introduction: This could be improved by adding that the production of consumer goods was much neglected in the 1930s.

Conclusion: This could be improved by adding that, economically, collectivisation was disastrous and, by 1941, agriculture had barely reached 1928 levels of production.

Page 65, Summarise the arguments

There were several reasons for the government's policy, from the mid-1930s, to strengthen the family. It was partly a response to the famine, to the drop in birth rate and the increase in divorce; also to the new elites' wish for bourgeois respectability, which the traditional family represented. Above all, it was a recognition of the need to increase the birth rate in order to sustain a strong military, big enough to compete with regimes like that of Nazi Germany, which were already increasing their own birth rates.

Page 65, Use own knowledge to support or contradict

Main argument: The Revolution gave power to the workers through their promotion to become managers, officials or replacements for the 'class enemies' who had been purged.

Counter-argument: However, it was still only a minority of workers for whom the Revolution had fulfilled its promises. Most continued to endure harsh living and working conditions.

Page 67, Complete the paragraph

... under Lenin, writers were not forced to conform whereas, under Stalin, they came under huge pressure to produce socialist realist art. However, not all did conform, so Stalin only achieved partial success in coercing all writers and artists to serve what he saw as the needs of the state.

Page 71, How far do you agree?

A ruthless government and an enthusiastic workforce had enabled the Soviet Union to industrialise in just over a decade, so much so that the country was able to withstand the Nazi onslaught from 1941 onwards. This suggested that there were no limits to what the Soviet Union could achieve. However, although the peasantry might have been 'conquered', they had not become more productive, while much of what was produced in industry was of poor quality. Meanwhile, in the localities, a huge number of 'little Stalins', supported by an increasing number of working-class party activists, achieved what both they and the leadership wanted: a socialist revolution. However, the Revolution, as the reference to 'little Stalins' hints, established a very personal, Stalinist dictatorship which could be reversed when Stalin died or was removed. Furthermore, it can be argued that many of the 'little Stalins' constituted an elite who enjoyed the privileges of a bourgeoisie, which they claimed to have removed, suggesting that the Revolution was not as irreversible as it might appear.

Section 4: The Stalinist dictatorship and reaction, 1941–64

Page 75, How far do you agree?

Main arguments:

Like an 'absolute monarch', adored by his people, Stalin believed that he knew what was best for party and people.

The suffering at the hands of the German invaders was exacerbated by Stalin's poor decisions and the terror he inflicted on his own people.

To avoid Stalin's 'savagery', the people drew on their reserves of courage and resilience.

Critical comments:

As in the years before the war, Stalin's power was unlimited and major decisions, sometimes bad ones, were all his. He did, however, increasingly leave conduct of the war to his generals.

It is an exaggeration to say that Stalin's mistakes were as much to blame for the suffering of the people as the impact of German forces, even though over a million of those from ethnic minorities were uprooted wholesale on Stalin's orders.

The German invasion led to the deaths of many millions. Stalin's 'savagery', for example in dealing with 'cowards' at the front line, led to the execution of thousands, not millions.

The Soviet people, perhaps inured to hardship by their experience of collectivisation, industrialisation and the purges in the 1930s, showed yet again how much pain and suffering they could endure in a collective effort to defend the motherland.

Page 75, Developing an argument

Stalin continued to make use of terror as a method of government during the war although the targets of his terror were less likely to be peasants and party members, as they had been in the 1930s. Instead, terror was used on the front line at Stalingrad, for example, in order to deter soldiers from retreating. It was also exploited in the transfer of ethnic minorities, such as Germans and Ukrainians, who might, in Stalin's view, form a fifth column and fight alongside the invading German forces. Thus, Stalin carried on exploiting the use of terror during the war.

Page 77, Use own knowledge to support or contradict

Interpretation offered by the extract: The Germans' brutal treatment of Russians in the war made it much easier for the Soviet government to maintain the support of its people and thus win the war.

Counter-argument: The strength of national feeling meant that the Russians were prepared to make huge sacrifices in order to defend their motherland.

Page 77, Turning assertion into argument

... It was even further emphasised with a huge increase in spending on arms.

... Thousands of factories were moved and new ones built beyond the reach of invading forces, thus developing the Urals and regions beyond.

... The working day became longer and harsher punishments were introduced for lateness and absenteeism.

... This was because many men had been drafted into the army and industry.

... The churches had been suppressed before the war but were now allowed to reopen and play their part in raising morale and support for defence of holy Mother Russia.

Page 79, Develop the detail

... Acting like a 'Red Tsar', Stalin ordered the execution of some old Bolshevik leaders, accusing them of spying for Western powers, while Poles, Germans and Ukrainians were moved, on Stalin's orders, because of his suspicion that they might join invading forces.

... A main reason for embarking on rapid industrialisation was fear of the capitalist West and what Stalin saw as its desire to crush communist Russia. Stalin, as powerful, autocratic leader, demanded harsh punishments for managers who failed to meet their targets. Both in the 1930s and in the war years, Stalin decreed harsh sentences for slackers at work in order to ensure the Soviet Union met its targets and became strong enough to defeat its Western (i.e. German) enemies.

... As autocratic leader, Stalin carried out collectivisation by force, using secret police and army units. The main motivation was to modernise agriculture and extract more grain from the peasants rather than fear of the West.

Stalin wanted to show that the Soviet Union could become a major industrial nation and that communism could bring about material advancement for the people.

... He had an exaggerated fear of challenges to his leadership and of being overthrown. He wanted to rule, with unrivalled and untrammelled authority, over a subservient and compliant people.

Page 79, Introducing and concluding an argument

Both in the introduction and conclusion it should be stated that post-war use of terror was on a much smaller scale than in the 1930s.

Page 81, How far do you agree?

Stalin left behind several problems which, if not resolved, could destabilise the Soviet order. His successors recognised this yet wanted to preserve the fundamental structure of the Stalinist system from which they derived their power and status. The unrestrained show of popular opinion in Red Square made them nervous and, for some of them, seemed to illustrate the need for a degree of reform in order to satisfy popular feeling and preserve Soviet society. The immediate release of hundreds of thousands of prisoners from the labour camps might be seen as evidence of recognition of the need for reform, as might the easing of censorship and proposals to boost the production of food and consumer goods.

Page 81, Developing an argument

Stalin was personally dominant, seeing and portraying himself as the embodiment of the party, throughout the years 1928–53. He inherited a one-party state with a secret police and made increasing use of the latter, for instance in order to carry out rapid collectivisation. As he developed his personal dictatorship, he resorted to terror as a political weapon, both to eliminate rivals and to purge the party membership, especially from 1934 onwards. Its use was revived after the war, especially as Stalin's paranoia increased, although it was not practised on the scale it had been in the 1930s. The cult of personality was developed in the 1930s, making particularly effective use of visual propaganda, and reached its height in the post-war period.

Page 83, Turning assertion into argument

… The war was conducted by a small team, with Stalin at the head. Soldiers deemed to be 'cowards' were shot and many returning prisoners of war were sent to labour camps.

… Stalin demoted potential rivals and rarely called meetings of the Central Committee or Politburo, and the cult of personality reached its height.

… Millions of political prisoners were released, censorship was relaxed and Stalin's use of terror was denounced.

… The KGB maintained an extensive network of spies and informers, while thousands of the regime's critics were imprisoned.

Page 85, Use own knowledge to support or contradict

Interpretation offered by the extract: Under Khrushchev, agricultural production, especially with the Virgin Lands scheme, increased, and the sector received far more financial support from the government.

Counter-argument: Although agriculture was undoubtedly better funded under Khrushchev, the higher production levels of 1954–56 were not sustained. The Virgin Lands scheme was badly planned and poorly implemented and, in 1963, the Soviet Union had to import grain to avoid another famine.

Page 85, Introducing and concluding an argument

Introduction: You might omit the second sentence and, instead, stress massive achievement of heavy industry and defence during and after war. The Virgin Lands scheme should also be mentioned.

Conclusion: It is worth mentioning that there was no sustained improvement in agriculture despite huge investment in Virgin Lands and other schemes.

Page 87, Eliminate irrelevance

The section 'Factories and steel works … were priorities' could be eliminated in order to maintain the focus on the living standards of the people.

Page 89, How far do you agree?

The two main reasons why Khrushchev was removed were:

His attack on Stalin undermined the authority of the party, suggesting that it might be flawed in some way.

He made unrealistic promises which, especially by the early 1960s, when economic growth slowed down, looked unlikely to be achieved.

Critical comment:

His attack on Stalin might indirectly have led some to question, even to doubt, the authority of the party and its 'monopoly of power'. By implication, this might have led Khrushchev's colleagues to feel that the basis of their own power and status was threatened.

He had made reckless promises about overtaking the USA in living standards. His 'naivety and impetuosity' had led him to initiate schemes like the Virgin Lands scheme, which were not as productive as promised so that, by 1963, the Soviet Union was having to import grain from abroad.

Page 89, Developing an argument

Stalin established a personal dictatorship and, backed by the secret police, was ruthless in eliminating all critics and rivals, especially in the party hierarchy. The use of terror was complemented by the cult of personality, which won mass support, even the adulation, of millions, by portraying Stalin as an all-knowing father figure and, especially after the war, as the country's saviour. Khrushchev revealed the extent of Stalin's brutality and dismantled the structure of his dictatorship by releasing millions of political prisoners and reducing the power of the secret police. He was ousted because his colleagues plotted his downfall while he was on holiday and they won majority support in the party hierarchy for their action. Neither they nor he resorted to violence. Instead, Khrushchev accepted their decision, confident in the belief that he left his country a fairer, freer and happier place.